RAGGED

RAGGED

SPIRITUAL DISCIPLINES FOR THE SPIRITUALLY EXHAUSTED

FOREWORD BY:
ELYSE FITZPATRICK

———

Gretchen Ronnevik

Published by:
1517 Publishing
PO Box 54032
Irvine, CA 92619-4032

Publisher's Cataloging-In-Publication Data
(Prepared by The Donohue Group, Inc.)

Names: Ronnevik, Gretchen, author. | Fitzpatrick, Elyse, 1950- writer of supplementary textual content.
Title: Ragged : spiritual disciplines for the spiritually exhausted / by Gretchen Ronnevik ; foreword by Elyse Fitzpatrick.
Description: Irvine, CA : 1517 Publishing, [2021] | Includes bibliographical references.
Identifiers: ISBN 9781948969482 | ISBN 9781948969499 (ebook)
Subjects: LCSH: Christian women—Religious life. | Spiritual exercises. | God (Christianity)—Faithfulness. | Discipline—Religious aspects—Christianity.
Classification: LCC BV4527 .R66 2021 (print) | LCC BV4527 (ebook) | DDC 248.8/43—dc23

Printed in the United States of America

Cover art by Brenton Clarke Little

For Sonja,

for all the honest conversations,
for dreaming kingdom dreams,
for continually pointing me to what Christ has done,
for sitting in anticipation together for what God will do.

"Now may the God of peace himself sanctify you completely, and may your whole spirit and soul and body be kept blameless at the coming of our Lord Jesus Christ. He who calls you is faithful; he will surely do it."

—1 THESSALONIANS 5:23–24 ESV

Contents

Foreword

I'M FINISHING UP MY 5th decade as a believer.

Honestly, that's hard for me to believe. I mean . . . how can I possibly be this old and how has my walk with Jesus been going on for so long?

Immediately after my conversion, I found myself in Bible college, where I learned first, how to locate different books in the Bible, and second, all the spiritual disciplines that I needed to practice so that I wouldn't fall away while becoming the person God wanted me to be.

For instance, I have memories of getting up very early in the morning and going to pre-prayer at school. That was the time of the day when I would gather with others before our Bible classes and pray for our studies, our lives, our church. I was part of a group of students known as the MIT's (Ministers in Training). We were the ones in the school who were expected to do it all—from street witnessing downtown every Sunday afternoon to cleaning the sanctuary on Saturday nights.

Within a few years, Phil and I married, and we practiced all the disciplines as we built our family together. During those days I remember having gone to a conference where I learned about listing prayer requests and journaling my prayers. So, I bought a special notebook for this task and filled it with every prayer request I heard so I wouldn't forget them. I would pray through them every morning—out on the patio, wrapped in sweatshirt and blanket—while my kids slept. Prayer was a discipline that I practiced regularly.

I also remember reading through the Bible every year. At this point I couldn't tell you how many times I've read through the whole thing. It's been a lot. I remember getting to attend the "Bible Readers Banquet" where Phil and I, along with others, were rewarded for our diligent reading. The pastor would give each of us a certificate that proved we were really serious about knowing the Word. Bible reading was a discipline that we practiced regularly.

I was a wife and mother of three. I taught daily in the little Christian school our church sponsored. Along with all the above, every time the doors of the church were opened, Sunday morning, Sunday night, Wednesday night and numerous days of "revival," when we attended special meetings, our family was there. Our lives were heavily invested in the church, in fellowship and in mutual encouragement.

And, I was exhausted. Actually, we were exhausted. I was demanding of my husband and children, and I was angry whenever anyone didn't live up to my expectations. I feared what would happen if I didn't control everything around me and if I didn't do "all the things." In fact, I remember one Saturday afternoon when I didn't have any work to do and could have just relaxed. Instead, I decided to sew an outfit for my daughter. About halfway through the project, I looked at Phil and said, "What's wrong with me? I must be trying to work off some guilt." I didn't realize it at the time, but those words were so very true.

There was, in the churches we attended then, but primarily in my own heart, a bent toward legalism, toward earning God's pleasure and fulfilling my destiny through my own efforts. I was utterly enslaved to the voice of the inner slave driver. Every night when I finally collapsed into bed, I needed to be assured that I had done everything that was required of me or I would make resolutions to "do better tomorrow." Before my conversion, I had lived a riotous life of shame, and I was determined never to go back, and never to let anyone I loved go there either.

Let's fast forward now to the early 2000's when I was reintroduced to the gospel. Through friends and gospel proclamation, I began to understand what I had been missing all those years: It was Jesus. It was His incarnation, sinless life, substitutionary death, bodily resurrection, ascension and reign. It was the absolution, the knowledge that my sins were forgiven and that I was then, and always had been beloved. It was Christianity as it had been meant to be lived. I discovered I was free—and that all the work I had done over the decades was really not necessary . . . at least not in the way I thought it was.

About now you might be expecting me to say that from then on, I put away the disciplines and just lived the way I wanted. But if you assume that, you would be missing the point. And that brings me to my friend, Gretchen's lovely book. What you're about to discover is that the life of the Christian, the life of the free woman or man, is not a life that's freed from all the spiritual disciplines. Rather, it's a life that's free to do the disciplines—from the position of being beloved, forgiven, and assured of eternal life. It's *because* we know that we don't *have to* do these things to be loved and welcomed by the Lord that we're able to do them with the right heart and the right motives—and they will bear the right fruit.

As I said, I'm finishing up 50 years of walking with the Lord. And still, most every day, I start with reading the Word and journaling prayers; of meditating on the Lord's goodness and seeking for wisdom. This book will be a wonderful guide as you also journey with Him. I'm thankful for Gretchen's transparency and her vibrant love for the Lord. You will be too. Enjoy.

Elyse Fitzpatrick,
Author of *Worthy: Celebrating the Value of Women*

Introduction

THE PIOUS WOMAN WAKES up when it's still dark. She creeps out of bed and puts a robe around her shoulders. She sits in her chair and lights a candle. She opens the well-worn Bible and starts to read the familiar words. Her prayer is eloquent, and yet personal. After 30 minutes or so, she closes the Bible, and gently starts to wake up her family to start the day. This time has strengthened her, and made her ready to be patient and pleasant for the remainder of the day.

That woman is not me.

I would love to be her, though. Some days I'm a bit like her, if I'm really on my game. I set my alarm to wake up in the morning. When it goes off, I press snooze about five times. I eventually get up, but the alarms have woken up my kids and an already chaotic day has now started too soon. Everyone is cranky.

On rare mornings, my kids don't wake up with my alarm. I tiptoe to my chair in the corner of the bedroom and open my Bible. I try to focus. I want to be good. *God, show me something. I don't understand this. This part is good, I guess. That's a good word.* I'll read two chapters, since things are going unhindered today. I close my Bible, say a short prayer, and then put a sticker in my journal on the "quiet time" line to show that I have completed a goal for today.

I've now ensured a wonderful day. I paid the dues.

But then children awaken and temper tantrums with them. Little voices interrupt each other and interrupt my thoughts. No one else seems to be as holy as I am, or care. This frustrates me to no end. I just need my family to get it together! The holiness hangover lasts about 10 minutes, and then I'm just praying for more coffee and wondering if my time would have been better spent sleeping. If "quiet time" isn't going to change my day, then why am I doing it?

For many years, if I got enough of these good mornings lined up, I would start to feel like I had mastered the "spiritual discipline" of being disciplined about being spiritual. Then it would stop. I would get sick, or someone in my family would get sick. Anything could throw me off this discipline, really: vacation, holidays, a late night out, kids, dogs, work, laziness.

I feel disappointed in myself again. *I just can't do it. I'm not a good Christian.*

I'll try reading in the evenings when my mind is more alert. Fail. There was that kids' choir concert that one evening that went late. I'll try during nap time. Shoot, they didn't sleep. I don't get my sticker.

I have tried bribing myself with scones, little muffins, a coffee pot by the chair in my room with a fancy teacup waiting for me when I wake up in the morning. I've tried planning ahead. It works . . . sometimes.

I am not a disciplined person. I don't even think I'm that great at disciplining my kids. And if I can't do that . . . how can I be a "good" Christian woman?

I used to think that if I had more time to give God, I would be more spiritual. But then I realized it was like saying that those who have more money to give to the church are more spiritual. God measures differently—as he points to the widow giving the pennies and calls her the most generous. What is this world Jesus described where the poor and weak are closer to God than the rich and strong? It doesn't feel that way.

This is not a book of wisdom nuggets. This is not a diet plan for your spiritual life. This is not a method or formula that will ensure a happy life. God calls Christians to faith, not formulas.

I hope this doesn't disappoint you, but this book isn't about self-discipline. I won't talk about checklists, goal setting, or achievement charts. Stickers don't sanctify. There's nothing wrong with practical tools; achievement isn't inherently connected with the spiritual disciplines. When I get stuck in the repeating cycle of quiet time, chaotic day, oversleep, guilty day, and over and over again it goes, I don't need a sticker chart. I need a soul at rest. I need the living God.

This book is for people who are tired and weary of charts and checklists, or more specifically they're tired of *failing* at all of that. They don't want to add to their pile of partially-filled-out planners. This is for people who are ragged. This book is for the people who are tired of the guilt and have started to believe they don't have the personality or aptitude to be who God expects them to be. Time with Jesus doesn't quite fit into the day—let alone is it foundational. They're tired, and they don't know how to fix it, besides mumbling a guilty resolution: "I should probably do better."

Sometimes we treat our time with God like a beautiful ball we would like to attend. We are Cinderella, and our stepmother says that if we just get our work done, we can go. If we just work hard enough, and don't misuse our time, and be good stewards and all, then we can get some God-time. If we are strong enough, resolute in our goals, and have the resources, we can get closer to God than those weak-willed people can.

But we do misuse our time. We do sleep in and forget to read God's word. We pray, but talking to him and talking to ourselves gets blurred, and we don't even know if it's "working." The needs and demands of others flood our day, and at the end, we are too tired to think deeply about spiritual things. So, we watch a movie.

It's our fault, or our family's fault, or our job's fault. Life becomes an endless stream of guilt and anger because of the dissonance in our lives—what we say is the most important to us doesn't appear to be the same on a day-to-day basis.

If only we could have gotten out of bed at the first chime of the alarm. If only we didn't have to deal with our sin, or the sins of others, we could be good, disciplined Christians!

Can God reach us—the lazy, the floundering, the tired—too? Or must we get ourselves together in order to experience the incredible grace of our Father on a daily basis? If we believe in God, shouldn't that mean we are able to do all of this? So, if we are unable, does that mean we have a faulty faith?

We have the best intentions. If the toddler hadn't broken that thing. If your mom hadn't called about grandma in a panic. If your boss hadn't kept you late at work. If your dog hadn't gotten into the trash. This broken world is against our carefully laid out plans. So why even bother?

You don't need tips and tricks. You don't need a new organizational system. You've probably tried many already. You want to depend on God and be a godly person, but you don't even know how to lean on God. Depend on God? What does that even mean? Does it mean sit back and do nothing? But what if God has called you to do something? Are we resigned to fatalism? Is it godly to be lazy and just "let God?" (I think the Apostle Paul would say, "by no means!")

You don't need permission for apathy any more than you need a flawless system. You and I need a paradigm shift—a fundamental reordering of our affections and approach to daily living that is oriented to the majesty of God. We need foundational, strong theology that provides us with a framework for all of our chaotic desires within us to get our spiritual lives in order. We need a fresh vision of what "order" looks like.

We need to know that the question of "how much time with God is enough?" is completely the wrong question, and we need to discover the right questions.

In the chapters that follow, we will discuss disciplines like: rest, Scripture reading and memorization, prayer, fasting, meditation, confession, generosity, mourning, and discipleship. These teach us how he is sufficient, and the purpose of growth is a *greater dependence* on him.

Must you do all of these things? Let's be honest, we don't need any more things on our to-do lists. We need more God, not more clutter. Most of us don't live the monastic life, but we do have vocations within God's kingdom, and people who depend on us.

I want to share with you many more ways God intends to work in your life without restricting your spiritual growth to 15 sacred minutes in the morning. God is working all the time and in various ways. When we recognize all the tools he has given us, and how he walks alongside us, the question is no longer "how much is enough?" Instead, we begin to recognize how holistic and practical "God-with-us" actually is. God is no longer a slot on our schedules, so we're not being graded on the size of the slot.

God often disrupts our schedules, interrupts our plans, and shows us the folly of our so-called quest for perfection so that we can learn once again that we are not performing for him. We are learning to depend on him, because that is where power and healing are. God will disrupt our striving towards our own ideal perfection as many times as he needs to in order to teach us to take our eyes off ourselves and look at him.

We will trip and fall along the way. But, because God is the one initiating relationship with us and not the other way around, we cannot fundamentally ruin anything. Spiritual disciplines help us understand our rights of adoption into God's family, which Jesus purchased for us as a gift on the cross and through his resurrection.

He didn't just purchase our salvation from Hell. He purchased the restoration of our intimacy with God. The curtain covering the Holy of Holies in the temple tore from top to bottom. Jesus made it so every trip and every fall would be redeemable. He has made it so that it all works together for good—even our mess-ups. I want to take you deep into the biblical concept of abiding in or depending on God.

Many of us live our lives on a quest for the things that will keep us afloat and un-rocked, like ship captains ever searching for calm seas. We seek after our own comfort for ourselves and peace in our relationships. We look for tips and tricks, for wisdom nuggets to apply to the spiritual sides of our lives. We are looking for rudders to keep our boats steady. We want our spiritual lives to be calmer and more efficient, to fit better into our days without disrupting them.

We stand at the helms of our ships, telling people how to steer. We want to learn how to make God listen to our orders, to keep our ship steady, because we are very well aware of how fragile our lives are being held together, and we have so little wiggle room that things just need to happen our way, or we might not make it.

But the paradigm shift is realizing that God is not on our staff. He's not one of our shipmates. He does not take commands from us. He's the captain of our ship, and not only that, the God who controls the seas.

Our works are just rags in light of his holiness, and trying to control everything has honestly left us ragged. We fear that he is in control because it means we're not. If we are totally honest, the idea that he is in control scares us.

We often want our sanctification and our growth to be in our hands—who knows what God will do with them? Can we not keep control of at least some part of our lives, Lord? We would like to grow in Christ, at our pace, keeping a close eye on our comfort levels. We know our limits, and we aren't sure God does.

These disciplines are not a substitute for belonging to a local church or from receiving communion. In fact, the very nature of spiritual disciplines (and the sacraments, for that matter) have both an individual and a communal nature to them. They should draw us closer to other believers, not to the spiritual individualism of "just Jesus and me." Spiritual disciplines do not call us to monastic life by ourselves. They call us to communal life. Life in Christ cannot be separated from being a part of the body.

Though we often wish God were a bit more concerned with our "happily ever after," and we are left feeling that the promise of Heaven lingers far off, God has a long history of bringing people out of their comfort zones and doing miracles through them. Often, painful miracles. Think of Job, Jonah, Paul, Peter . . . really anybody in the Bible who endured hard times under extreme stress that God allowed. And yet, in every case, he provided for his people.

My prayer is that this book will take you deeper into understanding what God desires for you, what he has given you, and how he will provide for you. My goal is to help you receive the lighter yoke of Christ, shirking the heavy yoke of perfection and performance, so that you may have greater peace in abiding in Christ.

I want to add that, while I write sometimes about my struggles as a wife and mother, this is not a book just for wives, or just for mothers. We each have our struggles, and while examples are given to aid understanding, it's the principles or truths that are universal, not my own limited experiences.

I want to say to my single or childless friends, your struggles are just as valid. Our stories might be different, but we are united at the foot of the cross. May our remembrance of Christ's works grow us in unity.

CHAPTER 1

God Disciplines Those He Loves

Storm Garden
Most days, I drag a hose
From the side of the house
To the backyard, but
Some mornings, I wake up
To find that the storm has
Already watered my garden

—RACHEL JOY WELCHER
TWO FUNERALS, THEN EASTER[1]

THE NEAT ROWS OF corn fields formed a dense green wall lining the county road like a tunnel, with a clear blue sky above. I was driving my five kids from our farm to Vacation Bible School at our church in town. A little black car was coming up to a two-way stop on our county roads. She saw the stop sign but skipped it as she thought she was alone in the country. At that same moment, my van appeared. Her car crushed my driver's side door and pushed our van into the ditch.

My calendar for the rest of summer and into the fall harvest season suddenly filled with doctors' appointments for myself and each of my five kids that were in the car. We learned that our initial soreness bore witness to structural injuries. Little ones heal faster than the big ones, though, and I had taken the brunt of the hit. Making it to neck treatments at the chiropractor and physical therapy appointments was nearly impossible with five kids in tow. Our extended family was dealing with some health issues at the same time with great-grandparents, as well as big life changes. Help was limited. Our chronic need required chronic help, and we didn't even know, at the time, how long our journey would be. As harvest came, my husband started his long work hours that are necessary to support our family.

During those lonely harvest months, I sank into a silent darkness. I became acutely aware of how incapable I was to do anything. It's one thing to ask a friend to watch my kids for one doctor appointment. It's harder to ask for help multiple times a week. I was the most injured, and yet it was my responsibility to care for these kids while enduring my own painful treatments with them as my audience. My brave face could never be taken off. It was physically exhausting, not to mention physically painful.

My "spiritual life" during this time was praying through emotional numbness, "God, I have three different appointments to drag all the kids to today. You know I physically can't do it, but it needs to be done. I'm too fragile to ask anyone for help anymore. I'm crying just thinking about how alone I feel. God, I don't know how it's going to work out. I'm just going to keep putting one foot in front of the other. I'm going to need your help with that. I'm going to need you to figure out what to do with my kids during my doctor appointments too. Just work it out. I just can't. My brain can't even problem solve, everything hurts." That was my prayer life. The Holy Spirit interpreted my groans.

I was scared that one of the little ones would break free in a parking lot, and I wouldn't have the physical strength to restrain him. I was still nursing my six-month-old baby, and as she twisted and stretched in my arms out of silly play, tears would run down my face from the pain in my shoulders, back, and neck.

How can I be a mother? What am I going to do? It hurts to hold them, to hug them, to discipline them, to put them in any timeout, to get them dressed.

With no fanfare, like a discrete servant, a friend from church would always meet me at my appointments to help out with the kids, or the receptionist would come out from behind her desk to show my kids the brand-new coloring books she got for them. She would just pull my crabby, fighting children into her lap and say what a delight they were. I looked out my window one afternoon and saw a cousin weeding my flower bed. Some mom friends came over with their teenagers to do other chores. A 17-year-old girl volunteered to watch my kids one day a week so I could have a day of rest.

I cried a lot during those months. When I wasn't crying, I felt nothing. I didn't take much time to rejoice in all the ways that God was providing for all my needs. I just knew I needed him to provide, and he came through. He didn't fail me, and why would he?

As my neck improved over the months and years, and my pain submitted to management, and chiropractic appointments and physical therapy became less common, I started to pick up the pieces of my neglected house, needy children and weary marriage. I did not resemble the pious Proverbs 31 woman. I resembled the man beaten on the side of the road whose wounds were bandaged by the Good Samaritan.

I wanted everything back in order, and my piety returned. As I continued to stumble in this pursuit, I prayed one morning, "Don't worry God. I'm getting better, I promise. *I promise I won't be so needy like this all the time. I won't always need you like this.*"

I heard the absurdity of my words as soon as they left my mouth. I realized that as I returned to my works, I craved that "independence" from God that I had before the accident. I realized that I had this idea that really "good" Christians didn't need God as much as those bad Christians. Good Christians didn't struggle with sin. They weren't so needy. They used biblical principles to pull themselves up by their bootstraps.

My pain didn't cause me to lose my temper or lash out, or not measure up as a wife and mother. It just removed any pretense I clung to previously that I was doing fine.

My prayer showed me that I had attempted to meld a desire to live independently and sufficiently of my own merits, to the theology that I am a broken sinner who is in desperate need of Christ daily. It doesn't work.

Spiritual maturity isn't pious independence from God, but a deeper dependence on him. The Christian life is to sink into his sufficiency, not prove we can do it on our own.

When I realized how independently I was trying to live my life, I started seeing how much I had taken upon myself to prove to myself and others that I was holy.

I started to spend a lot of time just sitting and reflecting on how incredibly needy I am. I became desperate to get more of God in my life . . . more of God's word in my life.

I felt like I burdened God with my neediness. I was ashamed of my need. The deeper I study God's word, the more I understand that God is exposing my neediness to my own eyes, so that I will depend on him. It's not something he begrudgingly does. It's the goal he is trying to push me towards. Total dependence on him restores us.

There are parallels to what I now recognize as trauma in my own life and the spiritual trauma sin has on one's life. In the case of trauma, we can be removed from the physical danger, but the brain and the body don't always recognize that the danger is gone. I have to retrain my brain to not trigger the stress hormone which triggers the rapid heartbeat, which triggers the panicked breathing every time I see a blue sky when the corn is tall and deep green like it was that summer of pain. I am no longer physically in danger. My brain is not convinced. That's why I needed to form new pathways in the brain to respond differently.

It is so with our souls. We are justified because of Jesus' work of a perfect life and a sacrificial death in our place on the cross. We are out of danger from hell. We are moved into the safety of God's eternal presence. But our hearts are not always convinced, and God knows this. That's why, through his kindness, we are given sanctification. It's our treatment to retrain our brains of the present reality of our salvation.

Dependence on God is the goal because it's living aligned with reality. When we are in Christ, being in the family of God is our true reality. Sanctification looks like leaning more heavily on God's strength than our own.

Dependence in Good Times and Bad

Whenever the subject of spiritual disciplines comes up, inevitably the illustration of the athlete often does as well. "Let us run the race with perseverance," Hebrews 12 tells us. But how do we get that perseverance? Do we will it out of ourselves? James 1:2–4 tells us, "Consider it pure joy, my brothers and sisters, whenever you face trials of many kinds, because you know that the testing of your faith produces perseverance. Let perseverance finish its work so that you may be mature and complete, not lacking anything."

We don't develop perseverance by conjuring it up within ourselves. God gave us the faith (Heb. 12:2, Eph. 2:8). God will test that faith, not to prove it genuine (after all, he is the one who gave it to us, and he doesn't hand out false gifts.) He tests it so that we may develop perseverance, which will work sanctification in us. This faith that he gave us, he will test, as we merely face the circumstances and trials, or the circumstances that God has allowed or even put in our lives.

In other words, living in this broken world will test our faith. Seeing God at work, time and time again, will mature our faith, as we learn to anticipate God doing his work.

> "For the Lord disciplines the one he loves, and chastises every son whom he receives. It is for the discipline that you have to endure. God is treating you as sons. For what son is there whom the father does not discipline? If you are left without discipline, in which all have participated, then you are illegitimate children and not sons. Besides this, we have had earthly fathers who disciplined us and we respected them. Shall we not much more be subject to the Father of spirits and live? For they disciplined us for a short time as it seemed best to them, but he disciplines us for our good, that we may share his holiness. For the moment all discipline seems painful rather than pleasant, but later it yields the peaceful fruit of righteousness to those who have been trained by it." (Heb. 12:6–11, ESV)

Discipline doesn't mean punishment. Jesus took all of our punishment upon himself. Discipline is training, provided by God, for our good, training us to understand our rights and freedoms as his child. It is not something that earns our favor with God. Rather, it is participating in relationship with him as his child. It is a sign of our restoration, not pre-qualification of our restoration.

Spiritual Disciplines

The spiritual disciplines repeat God's gospel story in our lives. They're an action taught in Scripture for the purpose of remembering what God has done, so that we depend on him rather than ourselves. "From a theological point of view worship constitutes the gospel in motion."[2] If our whole lives are worship, then the message of the gospel—Christ crucified for our sins and resurrected from the dead—will be in motion upon our lives, replayed from every angle.

The spiritual disciplines are the holy-therapy exercises to ground us in the reality of God's sufficient work. They are the recovery work on our human souls traumatized by the Fall (Gen. 3). They don't earn us grace. They awaken us to the reality of grace.

- **Rest** disciplines our minds so that we see that we are not the savior of ourselves.
- **Scripture reading and memorization** disciplines us in the vocabulary that the Holy Spirit speaks to grow our faith, and it replays the gospel story from the source.
- **Prayer** disciplines us to reach out to God and offers us a hallowed place to wrestle with hard questions that might undermine our faith. In prayer, we receive the access to the Holy of Holies that Christ's death on the cross purchased for us.
- **Fasting** disciplines us to know that God is sufficient in all we lack.

- **Meditation** disciplines our reason and imagination to understand the depth of God's love.
- **Confession** disciplines us to not hide anything from God, that we may find shelter in the light with him and thereby live out our restoration from sin.
- **Generosity** disciplines us to have an eternal kingdom mindset and not be overwhelmed by the temptations of the world that will leave us feeling empty. It also trains our eyes to see the needs of others and trains our hearts to act compassionately by default.
- **Lament** disciplines us to share our hurts with God, understanding that he does not expect us to pretend that our world is whole, and gives us opportunities to feel the practical comfort from the Holy Spirit repetitively.
- **Discipleship** disciplines us to engage hard questions, to live in the remembrance of what God has done for us, and thereby helps us understand the depth and longevity of faith that God gives.

God works our spiritual muscles through these disciplines. Just like much of physical therapy is passive, as the therapist pushes on the muscle of a patient whose job is to endure as it stretches, or to move a leg or shoulder when it hurts, sanctification disciplines our hearts that have the scar tissue of sin. Until we have new bodies in the new heaven and the new earth, we will carry this scar tissue. Sanctification means God will address the pain and soreness of this as well. He will help us endure.

We are accustomed to depending on God, or using these spiritual muscle exercises, when we are in a painful situation. When your child is sick in the hospital, you pray, and you ask others to pray. We see other's suffering in the hospital and give money to charity. Then we notice opportunities to witness to others in the hospital and start to experience the comfort of the Lord as we see his hand in all of this. We all know those types of hard circumstances, and inspiring stories of those who have learned to depend on God when he is their only hope.

Those who have been through deep valleys of pain and have seen the faithfulness of God know this well. However, there are some who grow up protected from a lot of trials. Also, there are seasons where life is good and steady. Maybe your life is beautiful. Maybe you have the house and the job you love. Maybe everything is going fine . . . and you can't enjoy it.

You can't help but wonder when God will take it all away. You hear of things happening to others, and you hold your kids tighter. Sicknesses spread, and you pray it passes by your house. Your prayers are along the lines of, "Please no. Please don't test us. Please don't make me trust you. God, I'm scared of what it will do to us if you are determined to grow us."

You hold onto this fear that any day, it will be your turn for tragedy to hit your family.

You frantically thank God daily to show him you are sanctified enough. You follow God's law as perfectly as you can, as an insurance policy. After all, there's wisdom in God's law, and you're determined to do your part to keep your life together. You reason that if you can prove yourself a good enough Christian, God will keep the trials that prove our faith away from us.

You believe in the gospel of Christ's finished work, sure. You believe in God's sufficiency, sure. But you sure hope you never have to use it. Even in these times of quiet, God is also working a spiritual muscle, and it's worked in the exact same way that he works it in times of trial. He invites you to fix your eyes on him and trust. How do we trust? We remember what he has done.

"Do this in remembrance of me." These were Christ's words at the Last Supper.

Not "do this to please me." Not "do this to prove you love me." Not "do this so I won't do something worse to you."

We will never reach a point in our Christian life where we won't need to remember our weakness and God's complete sufficiency. It is the song that plays on repeat throughout Scripture. Remembrance of that fact is our physical therapy. It's our discipline—a sign of the certainty of our redemption. Like the occupational therapists who can form new pathways of the brain to help the brain properly store memories through physical exercises, the spiritual disciplines are God putting us in physical situations where we must face our depravity and his sufficiency. Through that, we learn the fullness of our access to his strength that he gifted us freely.

Consider the Brothers

In Luke 15, Jesus tells a story about a prodigal son who asked for his inheritance prematurely, wasted it on the world, nearly starved to death, and came home to his father. He asked his father if he could be a servant, and at least stay alive. The father threw a party and restored him to the family.

The part of that story that has always convicted me was the older brother. He's annoyed that his younger, foolish brother gets such a celebration. He had done all the right things. His father never threw a party for him. I relate more to this brother. Too often, I feel like God owes me something for my good behavior.

Neither brother really grasped the freedom they had with their father. Neither brother realized that what the father was offering them was to partake in all that he had, whenever they wanted.

I think if this parable was told in today's culture, we would view the younger son as at least someone who takes some initiative and moves out of the house. The older brother would be the lazy millennial who never moves out. We raise our children to be independent. We want them to be self-sufficient.

It wasn't until I moved out to my husband's family farm that I realized that in an agrarian culture, you don't raise your children to leave. You raise them to stay. If they choose to be dependent on the farm, that means that they are choosing to live on their inheritance in a way that does not exploit it.

In an agrarian culture, you want your children to stay on the farm. You don't want them moving away to the city. I'm sure the father in the story was much like my husband's family, where the last thing you want to do is pressure and guilt the children to stay. You don't want them to feel like they are slaves to the land. You don't want them to feel trapped here. You send them off to college. You want them to see the world. They can leave and have their inheritance freely. But in the end, you wish they could stay on the farm with you, freely participating in the work, because they know it's their inheritance. God's kingdom will not be overcrowded. There is enough land to go around. He has a vocation rooted in our inheritance for each of us.

An adult child working on the farm knows they're getting an inheritance whether they stay or go. If they go and "cash out," the inheritance will someday run out. If they stay, they can live in and by the inheritance, even while their father lives.

No one works for an inheritance. It's freely given simply to those born into a family.

The younger son exploited his inheritance. The older son saw it as wages, as though he were simply one of his father's servants and not a son.

Scripture never displays the spiritual disciplines in a legalistic fashion. You won't find a list with details of how much, how long, or how often you must practice meditation, or prayer, or lament. They're just a part of life. The Holy Spirit will offer these things to you for each situation, as needed. He calls us to participate in our restoration, not contribute to our restoration.

We are restored when we remember what God has done, in very tangible, tactile ways. The restoration isn't theoretical. It's practical.

CHAPTER 2

Christ Is Always the Way

Blessed are the poor in spirit, for theirs is the kingdom of heaven.
Blessed are those who mourn, for they shall be comforted.
Blessed are the meek, for they shall inherit the earth.
Blessed are those who hunger and thirst for righteousness, for
   they shall be satisfied.

—MATTHEW 5:3–6 (ESV)

JESUS LOVES THE NEEDY. God himself stooped down to seek and
save what was lost (Luke 19:10). Jesus meets you in your need. "Jesus
is looking specifically for the people who can't get their act together."[1]
You cannot save yourself.

Everything about the spiritual disciplines starts from those realities. If you have your life together, and you don't need any help, and
you're interested in just polishing up here and there, you're going to
have a tough time understanding why God came at all, which is the
crux of Christianity.

A rich spiritual life isn't something we produce; it comes, but
from a source outside of us. We were made with lungs formed of dirt,
and the air we breathe is given from God.

In any kind of goal setting, you first assess where you are, and where you would like to be. Then you come up with some measurable benchmarks to track your progress. Then you celebrate and reward yourself with each passing benchmark.

When it comes to our spiritual life, you will know what your goals are already because they start with "I probably should . . ." Whether we get this list from the Bible, our family cultures, our church cultures, or just from the longings of our hearts, each of us has one. "I probably should read my Bible." "I probably should pray." We often name these tasks with the boredom and monotone voice of a teenager asked to do the dishes. Other times, it's an ache for nourishment that goes unfulfilled, as we try to hide our poverty. "I wish I could . . ."

When considering the long list of things that you "probably should" be doing, where are you now, and where would you like to be? I never asked that question for years. I just assumed that there was an ever-present "more" that I was not doing. I suppose what I wanted most of all was to look back on my life, and to know that I was faithful. I didn't want regrets.

Does the goal look like the monastic life? Or perhaps achieving a well-balanced life is the goal—having the right amount of Jesus, but not too much to get in the way of "real life." Where are we now, and what are we journeying towards?

The prodigal son journeys home. The early church was often called "the Way." John Bunyan wrote a book in which the main character, Christian, embarks on a quest to the Celestial City. We, similarly, conclude that "the Way" is somehow a road, symbolizing life, and we must walk on it towards heaven. This road is full of obedience and right choices. This all starts to make sense until you discover that "the Way" is a person.

Jesus isn't just helping us make good choices as he walks alongside us as our buddy on the road. Jesus is the road. Being on the road is recognizing every step is dependent on his work, his sacrifice, and his forgiveness.

Where Are We?

To understand what it is to not just be lost, but fallen, imagine something like the Chilean mining accident of 2010. In this story, a family is stuck in an underground cavern. They've fallen, deep below the rock, somewhat like a coal mine. It's too far to climb out and too far to chisel through in thousands of years, much less in time to ensure survival. They are trapped—this huge extended family.

This family has fallen into darkness. They didn't trip. It wasn't an accident. They foolishly believed there was gold down in the darkness, secrets more precious than the truth they were given. They thought there was treasure and knowledge that would outshine the brilliance of the sun, which they already had. They thought the shelter of the darkness would be more rewarding than the shelter of the light. The fall was more catastrophic than their imagination. There is now no way to save themselves.

Then light drills through from above—an air shaft, soon to be the shaft used to rescue them from this pit. The air shaft is a beam that shines a cone of white light into a circle onto the floor. The light is wide enough for many people to stand under, but several from all over the cavern just gawk at the light broadening down, illuminating the dust in the air. The light exposes the dirt on their faces and bodies that the darkness had hid. This beam exposes the height of the cavern and reveals how deep they've fallen with a dizzying effect. There is a love/hate relationship with this light. It gives the message of hope for rescue and shows a picture of what that will look like. At the same time, the light reveals the depth of the reality of how bad the situation really is.

They stand under the light as the wind carries seeds down from the shaft. This rescue will take time. The first priority is to be strengthened by food. Some people, with memory of such things instinctively push dirt over the seeds. Life quickly and supernaturally begins to grow in a place it should not naturally grow, as the light is that strong and other-worldly. A soft garden fills the circle of light. They walk under the light into the garden and look up. The plants reach their fullness and then stop, in a place of perpetual maturity. They can eat the fruit. They can touch the softness of the leaves just for the pleasure. They can use it as medicine. This supernatural garden cannot be killed, and it is perpetually sustaining.

At first, they look for the rescuer. What is taking so long? Is the garden the rescue?

The light gives an imprint of heavenly things over the garden, an eclipse of the world above. It is too painful to look at the light, so they look at the world above as a silhouette stamped on the ground. The family studies it, forms their whole culture around it, and reveres it as though the stamp itself had the power to save them. The imprint—the garden. Maybe this new way of life is the salvation. They worship this supernatural garden.

That is likely why they didn't recognize the rescuer who come down to them. He came through the air shaft. He would rescue them

CHRIST IS ALWAYS THE WAY

from being buried alive. He would not take them up yet. He came down to secure the line for their return. He actually knew what he was doing and made the return certain.

Even as this rescuer brought water, healed their wounds, and explained the uses of the garden, and how the details of what the imprint from the light shaft was representing, it would be absurd to say that the imprint from heaven was more valuable, or had more authority than the rescuer himself. It would be absurd to say that the prophecies of a rescuer hold more value than the actual rescuer himself.

Where Are We Going?

> "Therefore, since we are surrounded by so great a cloud of witnesses, *let us also lay aside every weight, and sin which clings so closely, and let us run with endurance the race that is set before us.*"
> (Heb. 12:1, italics mine)

It's the life verse of every athlete. It's the anthem of everyone who strives for a disciplined life; a commonly laid foundation for a biblical life of faith. The problem with standing upon this verse is that it starts with "therefore." Also, it appears in chapter 12, which is at the end of the book. This isn't the foundation, it's the conclusion, and not even the complete conclusion at that. Much is omitted when taking this verse out of context—all the things involving God.

To understand the "therefore" of Hebrews 12, here is a short summary of Hebrews 1–11:

The entire book of Hebrews is a clarification for Jews who had made generations of giving sacrifices in the temple and observed the strict Levitical laws for generations. Jesus had died and rose again, so, now what? Did they still need to follow the law? Did they still make sacrifices? You can almost hear the Jewish mothers asking, "Now that Jesus has risen to heaven, am I making Shabbat dinner this week or what? Is that over too? Do we still meet at the temple together? Do we still observe the feasts? Is our whole way of life and traditions of our fathers gone?"

Let's take the book of Hebrews chapter by chapter and see what each one reveals to us about God's vision for the Jews in their new era.

- Chapter 1: Long ago, God spoke through prophets, but in these last days, God spoke to us by his Son, who is heir to all things, and through him all creation was made. Jesus is the exact imprint of God's nature, and is not to be confused with angels, or anything else of a heavenly creature. Here, Jesus is identified as part of the triune Godhead from eternity, there at creation, not just a regular prophet.
- Chapter 2: Jesus is the founder of salvation. He who sanctifies, and those who are sanctified, all have one source. Jesus isn't just from heaven, he is a human brother, and a merciful, faithful high priest.
- Chapter 3: Jesus is greater than Moses—the man who received the law from God. The Israelites did not free themselves; God did. Moses did not write the law; God gave the law. Therefore, God is greater than Moses. Moses does not supersede God.
- Chapter 4: Jesus gave his people rest. He gave it at creation. He gave it in the ten commandments. He gave it by freeing the slaves. Rest and freedom come through belief.
- Chapter 5: Jesus is our high priest. He offered the sacrifice for sins. Don't sway from this truth. This is foundational for faith.

- Chapter 6: Jesus is a priest in the order of Melchizedek—that royal, heavenly priest named in Genesis who ministered to Abraham. God promised Abraham that his descendants would be numerous, that in his seed, the nations would be blessed. Jesus is a high priest forever to the children of Abraham.

- Chapter 7: Wait! How can Jesus be a priest, if he's from the tribe of Judah, instead of the priestly tribe of Levi? How can he offer a sacrifice when he isn't in the proper Levitical line? The priestly order of Melchizedek, who blessed Abraham, existed before Levitical priests even existed. Levi was the great-grandson of Abraham, so the line of Melchizedek comes before the line of Levi. Jesus' priesthood stands on a completely different (heavenly) playing field. Jesus started the priesthood back in Genesis and is our high priest now in heaven. He ascended into heaven, into the true Holy of Holies, which is the right hand of the Father.

- Chapter 8: The Levites had their covenant with God through their Levitical order. Jesus' covenant is greater than that covenant because he's a greater, heavenly priest, in the royal order of Melchizedek.

- Chapter 9: Everything we know about the earthly, Levitical priesthood was a shadow, or stamp of the heavenly, royal priesthood of Christ. Priests kept the genealogical line of Jesus alive, and helped us understand what it was that Christ had to do and how he would do it, through their priestly duties.

- Chapter 10: While the earthly priesthood relied upon repetitive sacrifices, Jesus' sacrifice ends that need. The sacrifice is complete. The old sacrifices only pointed to Jesus, and Jesus fulfilled everything that needed to be fulfilled. The old covenant involved our sacrifice, so that we repetitively knew that it wasn't enough—we'd just have to do it again tomorrow. The new covenant is entirely based on the completed sacrifice of Christ, and his covenant word. The covenant is no longer dependent on anything we do. Jesus' sacrifice covers all sins: past, present, and future.

- Chapter 11: We don't walk with God by our own sacrifices, but by faith in Christ's completed sacrifice. Look at the line of people throughout the Old Testament. Look at Abel, Abraham, Moses, Rahab, Gideon and so on. They didn't do what they did because of their grit and determination. They were all far from perfect, so it was obviously not of their own righteousness earned, but righteousness given. They did it by faith in the completed work of Christ—that they hadn't seen yet. They believed God was faithful, and God was capable, and their only hope was not found in their abilities, but in the promise of God. By faith we are saved, *just as* by faith they were saved. God is consistent. They were not saved through the law.

- Chapter 12: "**_Therefore_**,

  since we are surrounded by so many witnesses [to God's faithfulness], let us also lay aside every weight, and sin which clings so closely, and let us run with endurance the race that is set before us, *looking to Jesus, the founder and perfecter of our faith*, who for the joy that was set before him endured the cross, despising the shame, and is seated at the right hand of the throne of God." (Heb. 12:1–2, italics mine)

Chapter 12 is where the imperatives start. It's interesting how many motivational talks and inspirational plaques skip the first chapters of most epistles—the parts laying the foundation of the gospel (which is the completed law through the work of Christ)—and moves straight to the "therefore . . ." verses. We love to memorize the endings of the epistles, because that's when they finally give us something to do.

Chapter 12 is where God tells us to cast aside weight and sin. But this sanctification race looks different when you realize that the author just spent 11 chapters explaining that Jesus is the one doing everything, and it was for our freedom. He is the author of our faith. He is the perfecter of our faith.

What Do We Do Now?

Back in the dark cavern, once the light had been drilled, the rescuer came with his water, his healing, and returned above saying he would be back. In the meantime, he sent his Spirit, a refreshing wind that touched their skin and filled their lungs in the stale cavern. What use is the light beam from heaven now? The imprint remains, but the prophecies were fulfilled. The light remains as a visual representation of the heart of a God who holds the paradox of being both just and merciful. It is a memorial to what he has done, and a reminder that he will come again. It is the living evidence of all that had happened.

But God didn't leave the cave-dwellers with instructions to climb up after him. When he left, he told them to gather people from all the corners of the cavern, and wash them in the water, and show them the light, and feed them from the garden (which is the word of God). There are those who live in the dark corners and want nothing to do with the light and do not answer the proclamations. They still believe shelter is to be found in the darkness. They do not seek shelter under the light. Then there are those who see that the light is a route of salvation—by themselves.

People go crazy in places like this, even when the guarantee of rescue is proven. Panic starts to gnaw. Just thinking about the rock above their heads makes them quickly want to change the subject. People start to think of what would happen if the cavern just caves in? What if he doesn't return? What if something went wrong? Would he tell us?

Many compassionate people carried food grown in the garden to those in the darkness—carried them if they were weak. It's common for people to flinch when they come under the direct light. Some refuse to look up and just sob as they are washed and fed.

Still others, in their impatience, calculate how the rescuer made it up through the shaft. They can't wait anymore. They will scale the walls. They pluck leaves from the garden and shove them into their pockets or pin them on their clothes as mystical charms for luck.

The irony is, you have to leave the beam of light to scale the walls. The light beam touches no walls and shines in a low spot. Those who climb the face of the rock can still see the beam of light, but only from the side, with all of the dust being moved by the wind. It's a hallucination. The climbers think they are scaling up to the light as they gain altitude, but really, they are scaling a dark wall.

They cannot see God when they climb the walls, only the ray of light. They cannot look up into heaven. They cannot smell the fragrance or really have any comfort at all.

This light is given to us so that we see our sin, we see our need, recognize the magnitude of what Jesus did, and we see the needs of the people around us.

The ones who climb the walls die. You hear their screams as they fall. Even when some form groups and try to work together in team effort. They strategize, and the smart among them manipulate engineering techniques, but they are working with rocks. If they could just move enough rock. No, if they could just come together more. No, if they could climb on top of each other. No, maybe if they achieve the right balance or strength.

The higher they get, the farther they fall.

Trying to leave the cavern of their own strength, through the air shaft is impossible. But they can see it. They can feel it. It feels so possible. It's an illusion.

They curse their weakness and their inability. They curse God for taking so long. They curse their situation.

They were called to proclaim what the rescuer had done and said. They were to wash them in his water and feed them the gift of the garden. They were to care for others in the family. They were never told to climb, in fact, they were told to stay low.

The illusion of the climb is the weight that kills them, a passion that twists their mind. The calling given was to remain here and care for those in the family with the tools he left until his return.

The light is the law, which forces us to be honest about our weakness, our sin, and our broken world. The law reveals what is true. Trying to save ourselves by climbing through this light shaft is dangerous. Waiting on the Lord, and doing his will to love our neighbors, gather them, disciple them, baptize them, serve them is what we are called to do in light of the fact that Jesus fulfilled all that needed to be fulfilled. He came through the law, he completed the law, our future is secure, and now as a sign that our relationship is restored, he is letting us be involved as we were in Eden, caring for the world he put us in, but this time, bearing witness to the works of his hands, we will know it is all his, we are not strong enough to "play God" as Adam and Eve did when they ate that fruit (Gen. 3).

God never asked us to save ourselves. The law was given to show his greatness, not our own.

Where are we going? We are staying right here until God takes us home.

What does this have to do with the spiritual disciplines? God's discipline is about life in the light, in a garden of his word, grown for our nourishment. It is about remembering what he did so we never forget and sharing that with others. It's the individual remembrance and the communal remembrance.

- Remember where you are—in a world fallen in sin.
- Remember who God is—our only Rescuer.
- Remember what he has done.

Seeking the Mountaintop Formula

As I have a lifetime of goal-setting and desires to "go deep" with God, I have found that distinguishing law and gospel clarifies what it means to be both a sinner and a saint. The law is not a picture of my goodness, it's a picture of his.

Once you have been a Christian for a while, it's easy to forget this. After the spiritual high of knowing deep down that we are saved not through works, but by faith alone, we are a witness to God at work in us. That realization can be dizzying with its power.

Then the mess of the battle for souls around us begins. We still chase that high—trying to manipulate or manufacture it.

What was that formula we used for the last spiritual high? Should we try it again? Was it the music? Was it the prayer? Was it the people we were with?

We don't often understand that in the Christian life, "the high" is often given in low, hard places.

Some people recommit their lives to Jesus over and over in search of the high. They try being baptized again and again. They question their assurance. It becomes about their emotions, rather than their memory.

For some reason, when we talk about what it means to become a Christian, we refer to God's unending grace. When we talk about *experiencing* that grace daily, the conversation starts to sound like a business/success book with some self-help thrown in. We start talking about strategy, self-discipline, life-hacks, and the guilt falls upon us, because, before we recognized it, we'd started climbing in our own strength, and we started to believe it was enough to get us out.

We come up with plans for success. How can we become stronger Christians? We know the road will be hard, so we draw from multi-level-marketing companies' strategies for sustaining and reproducing the faith. Pump yourself up. Say the affirmations in the mirror. Believe in yourself. Do the work.

We forget that God came for the weak. Paul's affirmation is found in 2 Corinthians 12:9–10: "But he said to me, 'My grace is sufficient for you, for my power is made perfect in weakness.' Therefore I will boast all the more gladly of my weaknesses, so that the power of Christ will rest upon me. For the sake of Christ, then, I am content with weaknesses, insults, hardships, persecutions, and calamities. For when I am weak, then I am strong." Someone should have told

Paul, that his hard message wouldn't sell anything. Saying he's weak, you're weak, I'm weak, we are all weak, exposed by the truth of the law, and we were all rescued by a perfect, strong Savior who loved us when we were buried alive in this cavern, does not sell product, but it does align us to the truth—and there is nothing more powerful than the truth of the law and gospel.

Works-based sanctification, also called self-righteousness, is a vicious cycle. It's a weight that entangles us. Throw off the illusion and fix your eyes on Jesus.

> "let us also lay aside every weight, and sin which clings so closely, and let us run with endurance the race that is set before us." (Heb. 12:1b)

The weight, **the sin** that is at the core of all sin is pride.

"I can do this. I don't need God."

It was the first sin in the Garden of Eden. The sin of unbelief. The sin that took our rest. This sin of no faith in God and his promises.

The spiritual disciplines are an act of remembrance of God's grace, not a means of obtaining it or manipulating it. God made the covenant. God sacrificed his Son. Anything we do at this point is evidence of his redemption in our lives, and he will get all the glory.

CHAPTER 3

Dependence Not Achievement

"God doesn't call us from a place of need; we call to him.
We get the grace; he gets the glory. *And we never switch roles.*
If you do, you'll live a life of guilt-laden burnout instead of one
sustained, joy-filled, life-giving sacrifice."

—J. D. GREEAR
JESUS, CONTINUED . . .[1]

WE OFTEN TREASURE ATTRIBUTES that don't align with the gospel—
attributes like independence, autonomy, and pride in oneself (the
"good kind" of pride). We glorify self-sufficiency and self-starting
hard workers. When we talk about the kind of Christians we want to
be, we often list things we look for in employees. When I headed off
to Bible school, I had been through confirmation, I had been a star
Sunday School student, and I had been on three short term mission
trips. I worked at a Bible camp in the summer. I had graduated from
a Lutheran high school. I spent most of my teenage years preparing
myself to get into the best linguistics program available at a top Bible
school so that I could be a Bible translator.

I didn't realize at the time how arrogant I was. It was impressed upon me from a young age that God needed more missionaries. Becoming a missionary was a top priority in my life. If God needed missionaries, then I wanted to be the first to volunteer—to lay down my life for God. Missionaries were, after all, the top level of Christians. They were the super Christians. People wrote books about them, which I read like adventure stories. I wanted to be like the missionaries in the books. They changed the world. They reached whole people groups. They sacrificed everything for the sake of the gospel. I didn't just want to be a missionary; I wanted to be the best missionary.

Then one day one of my professors turned my world upside down when he talked about how I needed God more than God needed me. He said if we didn't understand that, we would fall on our faces, and he'd seen too many missionaries fail for that reason.

As someone who grew up in the church, had been trained in law/gospel theology, and had witnessed dozens, if not hundreds of people come to know Jesus in my short lifetime, this should not have been news to me. Yet the idea that I needed God more than he needed me felt like a needle piercing my flesh, and the gospel was injected, and it honestly made me sick as the idea spread.

What does this mean? Does that mean that I don't matter? Does that mean that God isn't grateful for all the sacrifices I have made to get here? What am I even doing here? What does "calling" mean? Every plan I had made for my life up until that point, I had thought was for God. I came face to face with the fact that I had done it all for me and my glory. I was puffing myself up and adorning myself with good works like a peacock.

Does this mean I shouldn't be a missionary? I wondered. *Don't all missionaries struggle with this? Maybe it's unavoidable. What's the use of good works if they don't earn me anything? God, what are you trying to teach me?*

I was 19, confused, frustrated, and, honestly, hurt. I dropped out of Bible school for a year and took some courses by correspondence. I didn't know what I wanted to do with my life. I didn't know what God was trying to teach me. I loved Bible school, but my heart was angry, broken, and confused by the gospel. It wasn't that the Bible school was bad. Two people standing side by side can both do a good work. One can be doing a good work with a good heart, and one can be doing a good work from a bad heart. I was the one with the sinful, prideful heart.

I was doing it all for me, and I had no idea how to fix it.

I had to stop—at least to pause and wait. Wait for what? I didn't know. That was the worst of it. But I knew I couldn't go back to the place where my pride was fed, to the place where I had straight 'As,' and my ambitions meant more to me than anything Christ did. I don't think anyone understood why I dropped out. My then boyfriend, now husband, became the scapegoat in the eyes of many people in my life, though I rejected every hint that he was. How do you explain that something good had to stop while God worked on your heart in quiet obscurity? How could dropping out of college (a Bible college!) be the will of God?

In hindsight, God was detoxing my heart. He was letting me break so he could make me whole. He was chipping away at me. It hurt. Over 20 years later, I still get emotional thinking about how painful that time was. There is nothing more confusing than God saying "no" to something we feel is best for his kingdom.

"But God, isn't sending people out as missionaries good?" I asked over and over again that year.

God was teaching me that the gospel wasn't just for salvation. The gospel is for life. We will never outgrow our need for it. Missionaries replay the story of Christ crucified in our place over and over and over again, while refusing to let the power of the story abate with repetition. Until I understood that for myself and understood my daily dependence upon the gospel, I was in no position to teach it to others.

The Uncomfortable Gospel

The gospel is offensive and is often considered dangerous for two reasons. First, when one is rescued from death, it is assumed that they were in need of rescuing. The gospel makes no sense without the law, which will always expose how far we are from God's standard as it illuminates our sin. The gospel is God's sacrificial love, unending love, covenantal love. He sacrificed himself for our *sin*. In this narrative, we are the sinners. No one likes being called that.

The gospel is a finalizing statement for everyone who tried to climb the ladder of moralistic behavior and makes the permanent statement that only Christ is sinless. It follows, then, that the rest of us are sinners. This idea offends those who feel as though they have obtained some kind of status through the law. And it, perhaps unsettlingly, removes the promise of heaven through our own good behavior.

But if God removes the carrot on a stick for good behavior, won't people become morally destitute? Won't more people sin, and therefore, more people get hurt?

It is not wrong to logically conclude that people will slide in their morals if there is no motivation for them to be good. It's logical to assume that people will wrongly take grace as a license to sin. That's a logical assumption when it comes to the reality of the sin nature. However, that logic contains two false assumptions. First, it assumes people who are moral outwardly aren't already morally destitute in ways we cannot see, and, second, it assumes that fear of damnation is a stronger motivator for moral living than love.

To accept the doctrine that we are saved by faith, not by works, and that we are sanctified by faith, not by works, we must also accept that love is more powerful than fear. If not, God saved us, and then didn't care whether or not people were hurt by those in the church.

Perhaps this is why Paul wrote: "For this reason I bow my knees before the Father, from whom every family in heaven and on earth is named, that according to the riches of his glory he may grant you to be strengthened with power through his Spirit in your inner being, so that Christ may dwell in your hearts through faith—that you, being rooted and grounded in love, may have strength to comprehend with all the saints what is the breadth and length and height and depth, and to know the love of Christ that surpasses knowledge, that you may be filled with all the fullness of God." (Eph. 3:14–19).

Paul declared the doctrine of grace through faith because the love from God is more powerful in our lives than fear of God.

If someone believed that people were motivated for right living through threats, then a healthy spiritual life would be spent dwelling on the threats and fear, thinking of all of the worst-case scenarios, and coming up with a plan to save the world.

If someone believed that people were motivated for right living through love, then a healthy spiritual life would be spent dwelling on the love of God, and not just the bumper sticker version of John 3:16, either. It would look like an ongoing, joyful pursuit to sit and meditate on the love of God, to memorize the love of God, to pray for understanding of the love of God, and to even become a vessel of the outpouring of God's love.

The spiritual disciplines center around understanding the depth of God's love, because that is where the power is. If there is any achievement in us, any hint of salvation or even sanctification by our own works, we are moving away from that understanding, not towards it.

The Apostle Paul says, "though I myself have reason for confidence in the flesh also. If anyone else thinks he has reason for confidence in the flesh, I have more: circumcised on the eighth day, of the people of Israel, of the tribe of Benjamin, a Hebrew of Hebrews; as to the law, a Pharisee; as to zeal, a persecutor of the church; as to righteousness under the law, blameless. But whatever gain I had, I counted as loss for the sake of Christ. Indeed, I count everything as loss because of the surpassing worth of knowing Christ Jesus my Lord. For his sake I have suffered the loss of all things and count them as rubbish, in order that I may gain Christ and be found in him, not having a righteousness of my own that comes from the law, but that which comes through faith in Christ, the righteousness from God that depends on faith" (Phil. 3:4–9).

Also, in Galatians he says, "For you have heard of my former life in Judaism, how I persecuted the church of God violently and tried to destroy it. And I was advancing in Judaism beyond many of my own age among my people, so extremely zealous was I for the traditions of my fathers. But when he who had set me apart before I was born, and who called me by his grace, was pleased to reveal his Son to me, in order that I might preach him among the Gentiles, I did not immediately consult with anyone;" (Gal. 1:13–16).

Notice—in this passage, Paul talks about all that he obtained through good works. And yet? All that he obtained got him nowhere. But then he talks about what God did—the subjects of the sentences change as to who is doing the verbs, when it talks about "he who set me apart . . ." "who called me by his grace . . ." "[he] was please to reveal his Son to me . . ." Everything changed when God did the things instead of Paul doing the things. There is no status to obtain through the gospel except that which is given: "child of God." The law can impress people with our piety, but it doesn't save, and it motivates only through selfish reasons—pursuing it actually grows our selfishness and pride. In Paul's case, focusing on obtaining salvation through the law made him a murderer.

In contrast, the gospel grows the love of God. When we focus on the perfection, death, and resurrection of Christ, we find life-changing love and power. While it may sound redundant to fix our eyes on Jesus continually and to understand everything through the lens of Jesus, doing so is how we grow in love. Living in this way does not make us morally destitute. It makes us honest. The doctrine of the gospel does not allow any sort of pretense that we can do it without Jesus.

Before humans even became sinners, back in Genesis 1–2, God didn't make us capable of carrying the world on our shoulders. That was always his job. God did not design Adam and Eve and say, "now do all the work so I can sit back and rest." God placed them in a position where everything they had, and continued to have, came from him.

Neither did God put Adam and Eve in the garden to sit around and do nothing. God often assigns work as a sign of relationship and as a gift. Work was good—a joy, even—for them.

Three Stages of the Christian Life

- Justification: Christ taking all of our sins upon himself, and giving us his identity, so that when God looks at us, he sees us just as if we had never sinned. We are perfectly clean.
- Sanctification: This is God's ongoing work within us. We still continue to sin, and he still continues to forgive us. We are growing and maturing in our faith.
- Glorification: This happens in heaven, when we will be released from our sin nature and will no longer struggle with sin.

Once we are justified, or once we have received this free gift, we move into sanctification. Sanctification is just a word that means growing in your salvation. Martin Luther defines sanctification as: "the gracious work of the Holy Spirit by which He daily renews me more and more in the image of God through the Word and Sacraments."[2]

It means the ongoing regeneration, or continuous forgiveness. If God has forgiven all of our sins, both past and future, then his grace and forgiveness moves with us into the future. That is sanctification. It's the stubbornness of his grace—the promise to never leave us.

Because we are not "glorified" (perfect all the time) as we will be in heaven, we still struggle with sin on earth. To experience sanctification is to live with the privileges of adoption, while working out what it means to be in this family, with freedom and without fear of the adoption falling through as we struggle. When you enter a family through adoption, the mannerisms are foreign. The joy is foreign. The food may be foreign. Perhaps even the freedom to be yourself is foreign. Further, knowing who you are is tied up with who you used to be—and who you aren't anymore. Adoption doesn't mean a smooth transition for the brain or heart, and in most cases, there is a struggle right up until glorification. When we are glorified, we will shed no more tears. The solution is love—unconditional, unyielding, perfect love. The solution is not to examine the adoptee over and over to see if they're acting like God's child, to question their worthiness. The adoption papers (justification) make someone God's child. Centering our hearts and mind to that reality, repetitively, is the picture of sanctification.

If we are to be moral in the way of love, then we must be honest that we are both sinners and saints. We must be honest that we still sin (1 John 1). We must be honest about our past. We must be honest about our present struggle. If a daughter went to her adopted father and said, "Father, I am struggling. I'm ashamed that I am, but it's true. I'm struggling to understand this. I'm struggling to do that. Could you help me?" What loving father would not melt at such an honest admission and pleading?

In our state of sanctification, we struggle. At least I struggle, most of all because expectations I have of myself are continually broken. I still lose my temper. I still can't be the perfect Christian. Maturity seems to take a long time. I'm so sick of my weakness.

A rocky sanctification can make us question everything. If Satan has his way, he will have us questioning even our salvation—as though God's love was dependent on our performance.

It All Comes Back to Jesus

It took too long for me to realize that sanctification wasn't my job at all. It's God's job. It's something he does. 1 Thessalonians 5:23–24 says, "Now may the God of peace himself sanctify you completely, and may your whole spirit and soul and body be kept blameless at the coming of our Lord Jesus Christ. He who calls you is faithful; he will surely do it." He who covers us will keep us covered. He who gives us his own righteousness will let us keep that righteousness.

We cannot look within ourselves to sanctify. We must look to Christ. Hebrews 12:2a says, "looking to Jesus, the founder and perfecter of our faith." Jesus not only founded the faith, or gave us the justification, but he also is the perfecter, or sanctifier. That is not our job.

We must look to Jesus, and the work he has done, and believe him when he said: "It is finished."

There is nothing we can add to what he has done.

John 15:4–5 says, "Abide in me, and I in you. As the branch cannot bear fruit by itself, unless it abides in the vine, neither can you, unless you abide in me. I am the vine; you are the branches. Whoever abides in me and I in him, he it is that bears much fruit, for apart from me you can do nothing."

God is not calling us to perform, or somehow add to what he has done. He is asking us to lean into what he has done. He wants us to know more fully what he has done. He wants every ounce of our strength to come from him.

The Christian life isn't one of accomplishments, it's one of dependence. It's not like God picked us up, brushed us off, and told us to run along.

You cannot live independently of God. Believing we can is the lie that harkens back to Eden. Maybe if we ate of this fruit and became like God . . . we wouldn't need God.

We fought against dependence from the beginning.

Jesus Came for Sinners

"And Jesus answered them, 'Those who are well have no need of a physician, but those who are sick. I have not come to call the righteous but sinners to repentance.'" (Luke 5:31–32)

So many times, I often feel like I cannot get as close to God as I want because I'm not disciplined enough, I'm not organized enough, or I'm simply not a morning person. I have too many kids. I have too much on my plate. I am simply "not enough" to be that kind of faithful Christian.

What God calls us to looks less like middle-class, stay-at-home-mom, American pull-yourself-up-by-your-boot-strap theology. (What even is a boot-strap?) God calls us to something much more global—something that applies to people who don't have our resources. It's as available to the middle-class woman as it is to a poor, African mother, or a single, working Chinese woman, as it is to an Oxford scholar sitting in his study or me in my kitchen surrounded by children.

Life with God isn't just for the rich, the able, and the unburdened. In fact, it's quite the opposite.

Why do we keep thinking that once we are justified, we are the ones responsible to get our lives together? We have not yet been glorified, we still struggle deeply with sin, and we are just as much dependent on the works of Christ as we were before we were saved. That is a truth that we can learn no matter our resources of time or energy. We are each on this road with our own version of the lie of independence from God, that must be addressed uniquely. The Holy Spirit sees our hearts and has the power to change them.

Just because God wants us to deepen our faith through the knowledge of his love doesn't mean that fear won't be involved. Fear is a reality in the life of a sinner (Phil. 2:12–13). Fear and trembling are a natural reaction to God's work in us because of his power and holiness. As I have grown in my faith over the years, I find that I respond to the Holy Spirit faster than I used to, partly out of practice, and partly because I know the exhaustion of wrestling with God over an issue. It's just easier to give into him. I have not yet learned how to tame the Holy Spirit to my will, but he has certainly tamed me.

The gifts God gives us don't always feel like gifts. They feel like medicine or chores. They feel like discipline. In fact, Martin Luther in his famous "Freedom of a Christian" which pounds in the idea of salvation by faith alone, also says in regard to the outer man: "Here a person must take care to exercise moderate discipline over the body and subject it to the Spirit by means of fasting, vigils, and labor. The goal is to have the body obey and conform—and not hinder—the inner person of faith. Unless it is held in check, we know it is the nature of the body to undermine faith and the inner person."[3]

Luther goes on to clarify that the outer person does not drive the inner, rather, what exists shows on the outside. The goal is not to effect change to the inner man through the outer man. The goal isn't to kill the outer man, as the Gnostics would have—to literally cause ourselves harm and literally destroy our flesh—but is to align the outer man to the same truth that the inner man knows.

In the endless battle of philosophers and theologians over the body and spirit of a person, Luther says that this inner person is "abundantly and sufficiently justified by faith." The gnostic heretic would say that the spirit is good, and the material or body is bad. Luther's approach was that our spirit is justified by faith, and our bodies are disciplined to fall in line with the inner man.

> "Through faith we are restored to paradise and created anew. We have no need of works in order to be righteous; however, in order to avoid idleness and so that the body might be cared for and disciplined, works are done freely to please God. Since in this life we are not fully recreated, and our faith and love are not yet perfect, works that discipline the body ought to be increased."[4]

God is sovereign, but he is also patient. What is the purpose of discipline? What is he trying to accomplish? Is God's goal to make us his trophies?

As a parent, that's a complex question. Do I want my kids to be good? Yes! I want them to stop making stupid decisions, for their good and the good of those around them. I want them to not be the bully in class. I want them to be a blessing in their community. But most of all, I want them to trust me when I say something is for their good. That is a continuous struggle for them.

Faith restores all things—even trust. God has not only justified us, but he has put us in a sanctification program of his design, with his timing, with his initiation, to discipline us—medicate, if you prefer, with the medicine that will help us.

"Grace does not forbid giving directions, promises, corrections, and warnings. Only cruelty would forbid such help."[5] Our conflation of discipline and punishment makes this confusion. Jesus has taken our punishment of God's wrath upon himself, and yet, he does not rob us of the discipline that grows our hearts to a deeper understanding the Father's love.

We are not our own physician. We do not write our own prescriptions. We are the patient being treated.

We don't need to earn God's favor, but he does intend to teach us about his love—because we have forgotten it. We can't come up with our own lesson plan, because we don't even know what we have forgotten; we don't know what we need to learn. We have blind spots when it comes to seeing ourselves.

We have forgotten Eden. We have forgotten that we depend on him for everything. We forget that he is God, not us. God works towards our remembrance, towards us approaching him, and with greater confidence. He is working towards showing us his faithfulness. He's working towards healing our memories.

Why? Because he has already legally secured us as his children. Now he wants us to remember that he is our father.

The spiritual disciplines are not always fun or an emotional high. It is also spiritually dangerous to approach them as a foster child who is unsure of their footing in a family and just wanting to prove she is worthy to stay.

We cannot manipulate God's love through any of the disciplines. We cannot pray enough, fast enough, give enough money, or read the Bible in a year to earn his favor. No, those disciplines are there *for us* to understand deeper and wider, his love *for us*. Remembrance of this love is at the core of each discipline, and as we abide in that core truth, we are sustained by its power.

CHAPTER 4

Enough

"Give us discernment
in the face of troubling news reports.
Give us discernment
to know when to pray,
when to speak out,
when to act,
and when to simply
shut off our screens
and our devices,
and to sit quietly
in your presence,
Casting the burdens of this world
upon the strong shoulders
of the one who
alone
is able to bear them up.
Amen."

—DOUGLAS KAINE MCKELVEY
EVERY MOMENT HOLY[1]

I WANT TO SAY this correctly. The last thing I would want is to have those reading this to read their Bible *less*. I don't want you to pray *less*. On the other hand, I want you, dear reader, to think of spiritual disciplines outside of the terms of quantity.

Quantity is a form of measurement, and we love to measure things. Measurements fit nicely into goals charts. Businesses love measuring success. We love the word "quantifiable." It feels so responsible and scientific. We want to break our goals down into obtainable blocks, to conquer them step by step.

The trouble with a quantifiable approach is that you will be searching the Bible for a long time looking for quantifiable parameters to define expectations and the answer will basically be "all the time." It gives us no measuring stick less than "complete" or "full." There are no fractions when it comes to devotion.

As we are simultaneously sinners and saints, the question of "how much is enough" has two answers: never enough and always enough. There is no middle.

To guilt people into some fractional standard that the Bible does not spell out is misleading at best and manipulative at worst. We cannot give parameters that we make up, such as "It is not enough to read one verse a day." Those who live by the law will rate themselves by the law, but those who live by grace have no means with which to measure themselves besides grace.

These spiritual disciplines are good and worthy. When we dangle the carrot of "better spirituality through self-discipline," are we not using a counter-gospel to get people to remember the gospel? Are we not saying that people who have more free time and have been taught proper discipline have more access to God than the rest of us poor, overworked, incapable, lost people?

The terms that God uses for our life with him are quite different. An overview of the book of Hebrews shows how the law of sacrifices given to the Hebrews was quantified because it was a shadow (Heb. 10:1) of what God was doing in being the sacrifice *for us*. It always had pointed to the work of Christ from the beginning. In other words, God completed the work of justification and sanctification *for us*. God will accept nothing less than complete. Therefore, he is the complete sacrifice.

Sanctification is not quantifiable, because nothing less than complete is acceptable, and living out our redemption is the act of remembering the complete work of God. Therefore, trying to measure whether or not what we are doing is enough is anti-remembering. It's forgetting that God is enough, by trying to add to his enough.

Remembrance is a loaded word, but every sacrament, and every word of Scripture points to it. Remembering is the embodiment of life with God. When we ask ourselves, how do we depend? How do we abide? How do we live as a Christian? The answer always leads back to "remember."

Memory is a strange thing. Scientists love to study how we remember, which is strongly connected to how we forget, how our brains store and recall memoires, and how our brains actually don't get full. Our brains have sensory memory, working memory, and long-term memory.[2] We are learning more and more how our bodies store the memories of trauma and how every cell in our bodies carries memories. When the Bible asks us to remember, it is not simply requesting a mental task, but for us to engage in a practice that demonstrates that God does not intend to redeem us simply theoretically. He will redeem us to the very core of our being. God's redemption is practical, tangible, and sensory.

> "Brothers, I do not consider that I have made it my own. But one thing I do: forgetting what lies behind and straining forward to what lies ahead. I press on toward the goal for the prize of the upward call of God in Christ Jesus." (Phil. 3:13–14).

The act of forgetting and remembering is how we press on. It is the call from God in Christ Jesus.

"'Do this *anamnesis* of me' says Jesus at the Last Supper. The word means 'memory' or 'remembrance,' but also 'recollection,' even 'reconstitution'—not just going back into the past, but a gathering together into the present."[3] Remembering is the brain's way of bringing what was done in the past to the reality of the present.

> "Remembering Jesus, becoming members of his body, we are remembered by him, written in his Book of Life, located where we can never be forgotten. The theme of remembering and forgetting is interwoven with that of the Covenant, our familial relationship with God in the Hebrew and Christian scriptures."[4]

Memory is processing of what we know to be true. The beginning of memory, or "taking in" of reality is rooted in language. We are given names, and we memorize them so that we can call to others and be called by others. We attach words to things, so that those things have meaning and can be stored in our brains. Thus, the work of Adam "naming" the animals was the beginning of our own memory of God. Notice, Adam wasn't doing the work of creating the animals alongside God, but acknowledging and attaching a memory device to them. It was a means of remembering the work of God.

"The Word" which John 1:1 refers to is Jesus himself, the second person of the Trinity. This is no mistake, or coincidence, that "the Word" is the connecting device between God and us. God spoke words, and the earth stood at attention. "But only say the word, and my servant will be healed" (Matt 8:8).

Words have the power to re-center our minds to the reality of truth.

God is our Word, God has given us his word, words have power, and all of this is tied up with memory.

Like Adam, we get to name the works of God and, thus, remember the works of God. In naming the works of God, we recognize that we are living in his kingdom.

Life in Christ was never about our works. It's always been about remembering his works.

Remembrance is a core theme of grace from back in the Old Testament. "Disciplined remembrance is institutionalized in biblical faith because we are called to interpret our present circumstances in light of God's known faithfulness in the past . . . Total sensory involvement of participants provides the compelling link between these significant historic events and the anticipation of faithful living; reverence for the past is merged with relevance in the present . . . a host of events and tangible objects ensured that people remembered what they were called to remember."[5]

Psalm 77 is a great example of how remembering the works of God is a source of transformative courage. All of the feasts in the Old Testament were a call to remember. It's not a work of ours, it's remembering the work of God. Tactile remembrance is multisensory, and it is flexible enough to be done by any soul regardless of ability, status, availability, or workload. The servant has the ability to remember as much as the master. The scholar in his study may remember as well as the mother nursing her infant. To remember the works of God is to live in the reality of your wholeness.

We do not act from a position of superior spirituality, but from remembrance of our need for grace and God's lavishing grace upon us. In fact, attaching any part of our worth to the act of remembrance nullifies the remembrance.

The Holy Spirit

When I was a little girl, I had a curiosity about the Holy Spirit. I felt that he was never given the proper attention as the Father and Son parts of the Trinity. People always prayed to "Jesus" or "Our Heavenly Father." Why didn't they pray to the Holy Spirit? Why don't we talk about the Holy Spirit more?

Growing up Lutheran, I always got the impression that we as Lutherans were fine, theologically, with the Holy Spirit moving people but that in practicality we distrusted the "wild card factor," as I call it. We love our liturgy. We love *sola Scriptura*, which is the theological claim that only the Bible is the infallible word of God. We don't build doctrines around what people individually "heard from God" outside Scripture. Both of those things are entirely predictable, and the movement of the Holy Spirit can often feel unpredictable. Or is He?

I heard so many explanations about what the Holy Spirit can't do, all in the negative—He will never contradict Scripture, He will never lead you into something sinful, He will never . . . He won't . . .

But what *will* the Holy Spirit do? I asked my grandpa this question many times. After all, he was a retired pastor and church planter, my confirmation teacher, and probably the most influential person in my spiritual life. He always had the same answer: "The Holy Spirit always points to Jesus." When I was young, I didn't like that answer. It was too trite and simple. It felt like a trick. Now we are talking about Jesus again? I wanted to talk about the Holy Spirit and all the flashy things he can do.

There's a tension, as though being "lead by the Spirit" is in conflict with "*sola Scriptura*" or the truth that we need only need the Scriptures. The reason for that is this—because we associate emotional experiences with the Holy Spirit: tingling at the back of the neck, goosebumps, and gut feelings. The root of such distrust is often twofold: we lack a robust theology of who the Holy Spirit is, and we distrust our bodies. When Luther talks about disciplining the outer man (the body) to align with the reality of the inner man, this is the reason why.[6] We must not ignore what our bodies, emotions, and gut reactions say. We are holistic creatures, and God does not reach only our inner man and leave our physical bodies alone, but neither should we trust our bodies, as they are easily manipulated by evil.

The Holy Spirit is not so cruel as to reach us through unreliable means. Here are some of Martin Luther's explanations to consider:

- "When I say I believe in the Holy Spirit, I mean that I place myself in the care of the Holy Spirit and trust Him to help me believe in Christ and live by God's Word."[7]
- "The work of the Holy Spirit is to call, gather, enlighten, sanctify, and preserve."[8]
- Finally, "Sanctification is the gracious work of the Holy Spirit by which He daily renews me more and more in the image of God through the Word and Sacraments."[9]

The Holy Spirit uses the Word and Sacraments as his tools to reach us. While the sacraments are a means of grace, what is the Word? The simple answer might be the canon of Scripture, but that answer would be incomplete unless we consider the Holy Spirit's enlightenment.

The Holy Spirit enlightens through Scripture. Many people have read Scripture with eyes that are not opened, and they do not understand. But even then, we must think bigger, and not limit the extent to which the Holy Spirit will use Scripture in our life, even if we didn't know what we were reading at the time. He will bring Scripture to mind. He will use it to comfort. He will use it to help us rest. He will use it to bring us to confession. He will use it to help us understand. He will use it as a tool to enable us to disciple others. He will use it to convict and call those in the community of saints to physically help us. He will use it to bring us to unity.

To think that the Holy Spirit works outside of Scripture is absurd, but we must also understand that he does not limit his work through the Word to the 15 minutes reading in the morning that we have the physical pages open. The Word is preached. The Word is written on our hearts. The Word floats through our mind. The Word convicts. The Word disciplines—all by the power of the Holy Spirit. Any "hearing" that is true, is rooted in the Word. We may not understand the path he has us on, or feel his "voice" is clear enough to help us to know what to do, but we can read the Bible and know—not wonder—that this is the word of God, that we understand by the power of the Spirit.

When we are discussing the Holy Spirit disciplining us, it will not only be an act found in Scripture, but it will be an act that will draw us deeper into Scripture. While our bodies are not reliable, the Holy Spirit is completely reliable.

The Holy Spirit reminds us. The Holy Spirit communicates for us. The Holy Spirit calls us out on heart issues surrounding the spiritual disciplines like legalism, apathy, doubts, and anything else that others cannot see. He knows. He convicts. He points us back to Christ, and his completed work on the cross.

> "All Scripture is breathed out by God and profitable for teaching, for reproof, for correction, and for training in righteousness, that the man of God may be complete, equipped for every good work." (2 Tim. 3:16–17).

The work that the Holy Spirit does through Scripture will not be stagnant nor just an intake of information. It will move us and change us. It will not just reach our inner person but help train and discipline our outer person to be in alignment with the truth of the gospel. To be trained in righteousness is to be trained in the Holy Spirit-enlightened truth of what Jesus' death on the cross means. The end result is an outpouring of love, not only from God to us, but into every good work that pours out on our neighbors.

Holy Spirit Lead: Testing by Scripture and Intent

Later in this book, we'll discuss specific spiritual disciplines that have historically been taught in the church, from monastic to layperson contexts. They are tools which are used by the Holy Spirit *through the Word* in a variety of ways. Sometimes the purpose is to train us of the extent of access to God that we have. Sometimes the purpose will be to convict us. Sometimes the purpose will be to absolve us. Other times, the purpose will be to equip us to love our neighbors.

We do not need to reject tools such as Bible reading plans, goal setting, or prayer journals. Neither will our hope for growth be found in them. Tracking will be helpful for some. It will be too big of a temptation to glory (or despair!) in personal achievement for others. God often puts a certain person in our path to teach us a new method that is of enormous practical help. God does not hold back anything that we need to be found in him. He will lead and provide for us. Does this mean that we should listen for a voice to tell us what is next? Do we sit and wait until he takes action first? Do we listen to our emotions that will tell us to go or move?

There is freedom in the Christian life. If you feel a prompting or motivation to do a good work, you don't have to wait for a voice from heaven to do it. If there is an opportunity to work through a discipline with others in your church, it is very possible that this opportunity was put together by the Holy Spirit. Also, God calls us to many things that are good, but our emotions don't *feel* like doing it. How do we know what is guiding us? We test the spirits (1 John 4:1). This isn't inspecting our lives to see if they are good enough. This is testing the fruit of any inkling, motivation, call, or opportunity.

The Holy Spirit works with Scripture, and he will always, always point to the work of Christ.

You may want to ask yourself: Does this opportunity root you in the reality of God's love? Does this program help you have a biblical understanding of the depth of God's love? Does this reading plan make big of you, or make big of God? Does this mentor point you to Christ? Does it move you to love your neighbor? The fruit of the disciplines is to complete and equip us for every good work.

> "And I, when I came to you, brothers, did not come proclaiming to you the testimony of God with lofty speech or wisdom. For I decided to know nothing among you except Jesus Christ and him crucified." (1 Cor. 2:1–2 ESV).

> "Indeed, I count everything as loss because of the surpassing worth of knowing Christ Jesus my Lord. For his sake I have suffered

the loss of all things and count them as rubbish, in order that I may gain Christ and be found in him, not having a righteousness of my own that comes from the law, but that which comes through faith in Christ, the righteousness from God that depends on faith—that I may know him and the power of his resurrection, and may share his sufferings, becoming like him in his death, that by any means possible, I may attain the resurrection of the dead." (Phil. 3:8–11)

As the Holy Spirit moves us, and our emotions and outer man feel the effects of his discipline to the reality that the inner man already knows, feelings are not our enemy as much as they are messages to be examined for their truth. We examine them by the truth of Scripture. We must not take lightly either, the community of saints that God has given us to help us in this examination, from the writings of church fathers to the discipleship from our own pastors.

To "know his voice" (John 10:27) means that when we feel God is calling or leading us, we recognize that the Bible is the Holy Spirit's vocabulary. Unfortunately, he's not the only one who speaks fluent Scripture. Satan tempts Jesus using Scripture in Matthew 4:1–11. This is when we must not only consider "is this prompting found in Scripture" but "does this prompting point to Jesus, *his* power, *his* resurrection, and *his* perfect love?"

The prompting of the Holy Spirit will be the words of Scripture, and the intent of those words will always be to point to Christ crucified, which is the outpouring of love in our lives. The Spirit is incredibly reliable in this. Any prompting by any other spirit cannot pass both these tests. Our emotions will sometimes be involved. God's work in our lives is complete, as he intends to enlighten not just our minds, but our hearts, our bodies, our emotions—the whole package. But he is gentle and patient with us as he grows us.

Just as our finite minds are limited to understand an infinite God, as we must try to grasp paradoxes and mysteries, an academic understanding is not the same as "faith," so our emotions are naive to the risks of believing outside of solid truth. Every part of us must come under the sanctification of the Holy Spirit through Word and Sacrament.

How much is enough? You can leave that in the hands of the Holy Spirit. When your desire is to know Christ crucified, the Holy Spirit will guide you to the tools, resources, people, and opportunities. We are free to approach him for help. There were many years when I asked the Holy Spirit to wake me to read the Bible, as early morning was the only time available to me. He did. (I soon realized that the problem wasn't waking up, but getting up once I was awake.)

I have had to ask the Holy Spirit to find time for me to minister to the younger women in my church, because I couldn't figure out how to make the schedule work. He did. I have had to ask God to even give me the desire to be in his word, and I have asked him to give me the craving that I could not conjure up on my own. He did. He is more reliable than me. The more I understand that, the more I ask of him. The more I admit my weakness and asked for his help, the more he did. When we have a big view of what the Holy Spirit can do, we will approach him for help in even small, tangible ways to help us remember what Christ has done because that is his very purpose of being sent to us.

The Spirit is reliable and has not left us to guess. We can know if promptings come from him by testing it against Scripture and intent. We are free to participate in that leading. Be wary of any program that points to our salvation by works, of God's expectation of building our own righteousness which he has freely given to cover us. The "training in righteousness" does not mean we earn the righteousness. Rather, the Holy Spirit will train us in what this free righteousness does, and the full access to God that it gives us. We must be trained as to what it is. These true Holy Spirit-lead opportunities and tools that help us understand the Word will grow us in our faith. "So faith comes from hearing, and hearing through the word of Christ." (Rom. 10:17).

If we feel accomplished in our completion of any discipline, any full Bible reading chart, any unbroken goal setting, and we become puffed up in our own righteousness, we need only to confess and be absolved. Our pride will often get in the way, but that shouldn't deter us, as Christ's blood covers that too. When we understand that each misstep, each failure, each distraction that we will do is already forgiven, we should not hold back out of fear that our pride will overrule his grace.

After my grandpa died, I was given some of his old seminary books. One was a tattered, taped together, annotated-many-times-over book called *I Believe in the Holy Spirit*. As I read through the book, I realized my grandpa, (who gave me what I felt was a trite answer of "The Holy Spirit always points to Jesus") actually had an obsession with the Holy Spirit. Reading this book, I heard his deep voice in my head, as he must have recited passages of it to me to answer my non-stop questions about the power of the Holy Spirit. As we consider what we should or shouldn't attempt in approaching the spiritual disciplines, I'll leave you with what my grandpa wrote in the margins of this book in curly cursive with this thick fountain pen:

"Your worthiness cannot help you; your unworthiness cannot hinder you."

CHAPTER 5

Authority, Privilege, and Submission

"A Christian is a perfectly free lord of all, subject to none.
A Christian is a perfectly dutiful servant of all, subject to all."

—MARTIN LUTHER
THE FREEDOM OF A CHRISTIAN[1]

DURING MY FRESHMAN YEAR of college, I stood outside an abortion clinic in Chicago, with a pro-life crowd of other Christians, praying for the women who entered there. It was my first time at an event like this. Some people held signs. We stood the assigned distance away. I had a pit in my stomach. I was uncomfortable standing there, because some of the crowd members didn't pray, they shouted, ready to throw stones at the "adulterous women." I didn't want to shout at these women, I wanted to hug them and talk to them. I wanted to look into their eyes and share the love of Christ with them.

So, later, when I had the chance, I volunteered at a crisis pregnancy center instead. As a volunteer, I went through intensive training. First, I would walk through various curriculum with women who had decided to keep their babies and opted to take some of our free parenting classes. Then I trained in crisis care along with the nurses who worked at the center, which involved talking with women coming in for free pregnancy tests. These women were terrified. Many wanted abortions, but just wanted to talk it out with someone first.

The women who did end up leaving us to go to an abortion clinic were almost always pressured by someone outside of them to do so, and did through tears of oppression. Sometimes it was their mother who told them they would get kicked out of the house if they didn't get an abortion. The woman (oftentimes a teen) was terrified of homelessness or foster care. Oftentimes their boyfriend, or even husband, told them that the relationship would be over without an abortion.

The "freedom to choose" quickly becomes "the right to force" when it comes to women. The women often have very little choice in the matter, but since it's made legal, others will say that's the choice she is required to make for others' convenience. It is the reality for many whom Peter calls "the weaker vessel"—like when pimps bring prostitutes to abortion clinics, so that they can keep working, or when abuse and incest victims are forced to have abortions to cover up crimes.

Perhaps it is an extreme and horrific example, but where there is freedom, there is abuse of the weaker. We don't "have to" be in God's word every day. We aren't "required" to listen to a sermon. You won't get in trouble if you miss out on some event at church. When it comes to women especially, that often means "you don't get to, because you don't have to."

When we acknowledge that it's not a "need," it follows that perhaps you shouldn't ask for help to get it. We're just talking about "wants," like a wish list—extras. Like candy.

And we all have been trained to believe that God gives us what we need, not always what we want. Therefore, it's greedy to ask for help.

The spiritual disciplines start getting relegated to those who are willing and able. The poor, broken, and lesser get forgotten.

Not only that, but many of us love to play the martyr. We love to be the one sacrificing. We don't mind. It's okay. We just want you all to be happy . . . and love us.

This is why it is so important that we remember that spiritual disciplines are both of individual, and communal importance. When one part of the body is starving and not able to eat, the whole body should feel it. In fact, as soon as we lose either the individual or the communal element of any of the spiritual disciplines, twisted doctrine and pain inevitably follow.

I once met a woman who was over 90 years old, named Pricilla, who had dedicated her life to women's Bible studies. Since she was 20, she had drawn in women from her community—advertising with fliers, going door to door, and telling people that they were invited to her Bible study, where they could hear about how God loved them. She told me story after story.

"What was the biggest challenge for you, in leading these Bible studies?" I asked.

She didn't hesitate a single second. "Childcare."

I nodded in complete understanding. Not much has changed.

She said, "No one wants to watch the kids, so women have even an hour once a week to study God's word without interruption. I would spend most of my energy trying to convince people in the church that women just need a little bit of time each week to let them hear the gospel. For some reason, the men never had childcare issues for their Bible study or prayer groups, no matter when they meet. But the women often can't go, because they don't have anyone to watch their kids, or they have to rotate who misses that week, or they have to pay a babysitter, and they just don't have the money to attend a Bible study."

In the 1960s and 1970s, there was a sexual revolution, and the culture told women that they could do anything a man could do. That soon shifted to saying women *should* do everything a man could do. As a swinging response, the church started defining biblical womanhood, and telling women all the things that they should do. With the legalistic "shoulds" on the culture's side, and the legalistic "shoulds" on the church's side, somewhere along the line, an entire generation of women got smashed between a rock and a hard place. The gospel was too often not even mentioned to them, in the name of constant clarification of the law. Too often, no one was telling women that their value and identity didn't have anything to do with their works, but was found as a gift through the works of Christ.

This is not new. Even in biblical times there was an ideal of what women "should" be doing. The message often comes strongest from other women. The message of freedom gets lost, because we fear that women will interpret "freedom" according to the word's liberal connotations. Freedom sounds like a breakdown of the family. Freedom sounds like women breaking out of the chains of the home.

One woman found in Luke 10:38–42, understood her freedom. She understood her inheritance. Mary and Martha were sisters. When Jesus and his disciples came to visit, Mary had the audacity to sit at Jesus' feet and listen to him teach. Just like every good church potluck, after the service the men often sit as the women start fussing in the kitchen to set everything out. Mary's sister Martha was annoyed that Mary wasn't doing her duty as a woman. She wasn't mad at their brother Lazarus, since he would naturally be sitting with their guests. She was mad at Mary—so mad that she (likely) shamed her in front of everyone. "Lord, do you not care that my sister has left me to serve alone?" (v. 40). Notice Martha's not just mad at Mary. She's mad at the Lord and questioning his judgment as well. Lord, why aren't you *making her* do her duty? How can you be overlooking her laziness? She's not listening to me, but she will listen to you!

Jesus' defense of Mary has brought me to tears more than once. "Martha, Martha, you are anxious and troubled about many things, but one thing is necessary. Mary has chosen the good portion, which will not be taken away from her."

Jesus called what Mary was doing *necessary*. It was a legitimate need for a woman to need to hear the words of Jesus.

Mary chose to listen to Jesus—against the approval of others, and Jesus said it will not be taken from her. In other words, Jesus wasn't going to send her away, and he would ensure no one else took it away either. Jesus didn't see the value of women in how much they served. He saw that they needed him just as much as the men.

I struggle to claim my freedom, and my right as a Christian to sit at the feet of Jesus, and I say I struggle because my husband and children always need me, and I don't want to disappoint them. I struggle to even say, "I'll help you in 5 minutes. Just let me finish this page." I struggle to say, "No, this is more important." I struggle to say, "I need help."

"Can't you do that later?" They ask. Yes, I do have the freedom to do it later, and we all know it. So, it gets pushed off, and pushed off, and pushed off.

My title at home is "mom" but most days it feels like it is "support person." I make sure my husband has everything he needs for the farm, especially during the heavy seasons. (Well, at least I'm supposed to. I'm not an ideal farm wife.) I'm "the person" for six other people's doctor appointments and waiver signatures. I'm the homework tutor. I'm the constant list of questions—do you have enough food, enough sleep, enough clothing? I'm the person who makes it possible for everyone else in my family to do things.

Sometimes I wonder, "Do I get a support person, or does it all stop with me?"

As someone who firmly believes in the headship of my husband and embraces my life as a stay-at-home mom, I do both of those things in freedom, and not out of legalistic rules. Well, I do fall into legalism when I think that my loyalty to them trumps my loyalty to God, or that my loyalty to them earns favor with God, or when I value those roles above the role of "daughter of God."

It was years before God taught me that even as a wife, even as a mother, I have the authority to sit at his feet—even if it makes people upset. I have been given that privilege. My submission to him comes before my submission to anyone else, even if they don't like the timing or shape of my need.

The freedom given is mine to use, not for others to use against me.

I realized that I used to drop my Bible reading whenever someone needed me. I didn't make anyone wait. I didn't want to ask for help. I didn't communicate with those around me how hungry I was. *I didn't ask for help.* Though I complained, I didn't *ask.* I had attitude problems, and anger built up. But I didn't confess.

Being a martyr sometimes feels more righteous than being crucified with Christ. Feelings are unreliable, fickle things.

Sometimes, understanding older women, or those who have been where I am, would help without me asking. They are treasures. But none of the people in my home or in my church know how to read my mind, nor do they keep track of if I am getting spiritually fed. They don't have the Holy Spirit's access to see what is in my heart.

The words of Jesus, "it will not be taken from her" burrowed deep in my heart. The high expectations of my family to be some kind of super-human would have to be torn down.

For me, I had to stop meeting all of their needs. I was called to love them and sacrifice for them. But by living fully within my design meant they would still feel the need for a savior—a need I was killing myself to fill so they never had to ache for God.

The Communal Element

There was a time when I had to stay home from church for three weeks in a row, due to an illness that was running through our house. The kids weren't sick for a solid three weeks, but someone in our family was sick every weekend for three weeks. Since my husband had some duties at church as an elder, I was usually the one to offer to stay home. Plus, everyone wants mom when they're sick.

That third week was the week that our church distributes communion, and it was especially hard for me to stay home. Knut (my husband) was one of the men at church who helped distribute it, so once again, I stayed home with the one sick child.

"I just miss church so much. This is really getting hard." I whispered to him as he left. He felt awful.

That Sunday when they got home from church, Knut took me aside and said he had something for me. As we found a small corner of the house, he revealed a small communion cup and wafer. Tears filled my eyes. "I told Pastor Mark you were really struggling staying home today. We decided I should bring this home to you." My husband put his arm around me and awkwardly said, "This is the body of Christ, broken for you. Take and eat. This is the blood of Christ, poured out for you. Take and drink." I've never felt so seen by my husband and pastor. I sobbed at their thoughtfulness with all of the emotion of a mother of ailing children who hadn't slept well for weeks on end.

Let the individual and communal aspects of the sacraments of baptism and communion serve as a model for how the church should work. Everyone has the individual need to be baptized, but they are always baptized by someone other than themselves. Everyone has the individual need to take communion, but it is given by someone outside you, as you meet together. Baptism is a beautiful sign of justification, and communion is a beautiful sign of sanctification. God sees us individually. God sees us as one body.

I abused my freedom by not exercising the authority I have as an individual to sit at the feet of Jesus. But abuse of freedom, it can easily swing to the other side as well—exercising our authority to the detriment of those around us. When spiritual disciplines become too heavily individually focused and lose their communal aspect, it hurts those around us. It's the sin of the Pharisees, shaming Jesus for healing on the Sabbath—looking out for their own interests of "holiness" above the pain of someone's body.

Martin Luther said, "A Christian is a perfectly free lord of all, subject to none. A Christian is a perfectly dutiful servant of all, subject to all."[2] While we are not subject to fulfill the law, because of what

Christ has done for us, it is good to consider the heart and purpose behind the law—God's heart for us to, as Jesus put it: "And he said to him, 'You shall love the Lord your God with all your heart, and with all your soul, and with all your mind. This is the first and greatest commandment. And the second is like it: You shall love your neighbor as yourself.'" (Matt. 22:37–39) To love our neighbor with God excluded from the equation completely misses the heart of God. Equally, loving God, but taking no care to what our neighbors endure also misses understanding the heart of God. God sees us as individuals. God sees us as a community. It's not one or the other: it's both.

Biographers of A.W. Tozer say that talk about his own pursuit of God came at the expense of forcing his wife to raise their seven children nearly by herself. He also piously rejected the monetary gain that was at his fingertips through his writing, but that came at the expense of his wife rarely having everything she needed to raise the kids and scraping to get by.[3] The story is not unusual among ministers. It's why many pastors' kids earn the rebellious reputation they do—they know they come last.

I often wonder if for every monk who lived his life secluded in a monastery, was there a need in the village where his vocation was lacking? (Not all monastic life was secluded, many served their communities well.)

We know it is good to take seasons to be alone. Jesus would often retreat to be with his Father. But it isn't good to remain alone. How then could I pray, "Our Father . . ." when it is just me?

Those who seek God to such an extent that they are permanently absent from the rest of the church body, in effect, can harm the body. Are they there to ask: Do you need help?

Is that single mom getting a break? Is there a person with disabilities in your church who doesn't have access to the same things that the rest of the church enjoys? Is your pastor getting enough rest? Does that single person in your church have a safe person to confide her confessions, and speak absolution over her?

The goal of spiritual disciplines isn't to hide away on retreat for the rest of your life up on a mountain. Those people have not earned an extra level of holiness—holiness is freely given—not earned. But if the purpose isn't personal holiness, but to understand the depths of what God has done for us through his perfect holiness, it cannot be understood outside of community. We are called to love one another with the love that comes from God.

Perhaps that is why Jesus always appeared annoyed when the disciples argued over who was the greatest—this ranking of people by their accomplishments which was a distraction from the mission. Trying to "get ahead" or "rank ourselves" is something people did with the law. Ranking is utterly useless with the gospel, as we cannot rank ourselves when we are all being covered by the same works of Christ.

As a homeschooling mom, who has a husband with a very demanding job, I was obsessed with people-pleasing, but I "sanctified my sin" by calling it "submission" and "service." I wanted to make everyone happy, be everyone's savior, and be able to say "yes" as often as possible. Most of all, I don't want to be the needy one. The strong ones are the most spiritual, right?

What I didn't realize was that, when others had unhealthy expectations of me, I would not get out from under it by trying harder and doing more. The more I gave, the more they expected. I got out of it not by giving more but by learning to "fix my eyes on Jesus." God's discipline is for my good, he had to discipline me to know when to say "no."

On one hand, we women can find that it is "safe" to simply submit to husbands or parents, as they have our best interest at heart, and to just do as we are told. But that assumes that husbands or parents are not only sinless but are mind readers, who know our struggles, our pain, or our needs. That is a heavy burden to put on them to be god-like. We must give them the benefit of communicating our needs.

On the other hand, is there not also the risk of abuse of freedom, of trusting ourselves to not make selfish choices, of "being led by the Spirit" as an individualistic 'get out of jail free' card for anything we don't *feel* like doing? Couldn't we just say, "God said I don't have to do this"?

What is the formula for when it's okay to submit to the will of another person, and when it's okay to say "no"?

There is no formula. There is only faith.

We ask for wisdom. We seek God for direction. His Spirit points us to the work of the cross. There is simply no way to navigate this outside of dependence on the Holy Spirit. His law is now written on our hearts. Sometimes we interpret it correctly. Sometimes we don't. Sometimes we read Scripture correctly, other times we unconsciously twist it to do our will. We are under the authority of church leaders who are also sinners. We live and breathe in this sanctification. It's where we learn that Jesus is enough, when we are not. It's where we learn that our identities are not based on our abilities, or getting every decision right, but on the faithfulness of Christ on that cross.

As we live within a community, we do not need to force feed others. In fact, we are in no place to demand how others use their freedom. We are called to submit to one another, not force others to submit. Submission implies freedom, otherwise it would be called oppression.

However, we are called to be servants who go around making sure everyone has enough to eat, making sure to not to forget the widows and orphans. Who in your church isn't getting enough to eat?

- You are allowed to rest.
- You are allowed to spend time in God's word.
- You are not the savior.
- The man in your life is not your Savior.
- Submission is good, as long as it does not supersede God's word.

We do not have the right to have an uninterrupted, perfect plan fulfilled. But we do have the right to acknowledge our needs. We have the freedom of relationship as a daughter of God. Submitting to God means we cannot worship people pleasing.

"It will not be taken from her" are words to treasure in your heart. We can freely receive and freely give.

CHAPTER 6

Freedom through Dependence

"Now the Lord is the Spirit, and where the Spirit of the Lord is, there is freedom. And we all, with unveiled face, beholding the glory of the Lord, are being transformed into the same image from one degree of glory to another. For this comes from the Lord who is the Spirit."

—2 CORINTHIANS 3:17–18 (ESV)

SATAN WILL CALL US legalists when we try to regularly pray and failures when we forget to pray. Satan knows which side each of us tends to fall on, whether legalism or failure, and he will use it to call us names. As we try to self-correct, he will call us a different name. We will never satisfy him, because the fact is, he doesn't get to name us, and our God who does name us is satisfied already on account of Christ. What does a spiritual life, completely dependent on Christ and not on our own legalistic ideals, (or sliding into apathy) even look like? We must hold the paradox that freedom looks like dependence on God and dependence on God looks like freedom.

This world gives us trouble. We cannot escape suffering. However, God does not hold himself back from us. In the Old Testament, it looked like God commanded the people to put the tabernacle right in the middle of their camp. He wanted to be in their midst. In the New Testament, Jesus came in the flesh, and then sent his Spirit who will never leave us or forsake us. He desires to be with us in abundance.

The Holy Spirit is not ignorant of the obstacles we face in being with him. When looking throughout Scripture for helpful hints, you'll find mentions, clues, and references to disciplines. You'll never find them spelled out with detail because God has a different plan for each of us. He has good works that he has planned for each of us to do. My devotional time might look different than yours. It will look different from a monk or seminary professor. There are two reasons why no formula is given: it would rob us of the freedom to interact with God as needed for our situation, and we would inevitably make the formula our God, and our work to perform. A formula would take our eyes off of the person of Jesus.

The Holy Spirit is not ignorant of our lack of discipline, however. He understands our frustration of not knowing where to start. This is where church community and discipleship come into the picture. It is a relief when someone comes alongside us and teaches us to pray. It is a relief when someone teaches us how to give, how to fast, how to worship. I don't pick out the songs for church every week. I don't have to decide the order of worship. I just get to participate.

Oftentimes, when I am most empty, the last thing I'm able to do is decide what to do next. I'm broken; I can't come up with a plan. How do I know what I should read in the Bible next? I have no words to pray.

Liturgies Are for Us

I have six living kids now, but my fourth pregnancy ended in miscarriage. My husband was helpless in the thick of his busy time in the fields—our income is so weather dependent. I had three little kids at home, and when we told people that we lost a baby, the condolences were well meaning.

I spent two days just going through the motions just getting the kids fed, turning on the television for them and going between episodes of weeping and staring at the wall. I felt foolish for mourning something I had never fully known. I felt foolish for making a big deal. I felt foolish for not making a big enough deal. Why don't we have funerals for unborn babies? Should we? I had no blueprint for how to mourn this. I was floating along in numbness and tears. How do I do this? How do I endure this? Am I supposed to be doing something? Should it hurt this much?

Then, one of my friends from three hours away packed up her two kids. She and her husband drove out to my farm. I didn't even know them well, but when she found out I miscarried, she just came. She showed up on my doorstep with her family, and her kids ran to play with my kids, as her husband watched them all for us. She sat and talked with me for three hours. Then they said they were taking us all out to a restaurant to eat. When we got to the restaurant, they watched all the kids, helped them order, and cut their food. They told me to just eat. They were intent on me eating my full plate without having to watch the kids. After my first bite, my body suddenly remembered that I hadn't eaten in two days. I didn't even realize I hadn't eaten. How on earth do you not eat and not realize it? I was famished.

There's a specific comfort that when someone cares for you.

Now eat this. Now go lay down. I have this. It's okay to cry. I'm here. Now I think it would be good for you to go for a walk outside. I'll read the kids a book; you take a shower. Do this. Do that.

These instructions weren't given to me as law. They were given to me as love. My friend, through her directions, acknowledged my inability to cope. She needed nothing from me. She just gave gift after gift.

This is the heart of liturgy. When we are at the peak of our exhaustion and whatever we've been doing isn't working, we need someone to intervene and care for us. It is a service for us, to be given something to do when we have no idea what to do. It is a way that others can care for you and point you to Christ. When liturgy is done well, you come away with the impression that someone was thoughtful or helpful. We don't often know what we needed, until we started doing it. That's often what spiritual obedience looks like.

I am encouraged by my church leadership, who has a service designed with intentional routine to point me to Christ. I am encouraged by a book of prayers, when someone else has written out a prayer for me when I have none. I'm encouraged by picking up a reading plan when I don't know where to start. These rhythms can suffocate us when we charge at them like an overseer with a clipboard, grading each person by their product. But they can also give us direction when lost, and they put our feet on something solid when we are beyond exhaustion.

It's often not the tools that are wrong; it's the "why" behind their use that gets us into trouble.

At first glance, liturgy looks like just a good habit or routine. You go to church on Sundays. You go to your Bible study on Tuesdays. You pray before your dinner. People seem to love or hate liturgies. Some find comfort in the regularity of them, and how they alleviate the burden of constant decision making. *The decision is made, this is just what we do.*

Still others find the rote recitations and days to be numbing. For these individuals, liturgies have lost their usefulness, or perhaps are not the right liturgy for the right time. They are done out of obligation rather than recognizing a need. But liturgies are not laws. They are tools intended to care for us.

The difference between a habit and a liturgy is the spirit of service, rather than the spirit of performance. In that respect, it is usually impossible to tell the difference from the outside, as it's more often a matter of the heart. We must ask: is it building up the kingdom of God? Is it reminding us of the work of Christ?

There is freedom in knowing we are not chasing after our acceptance. There is freedom in knowing we are not chasing an emotional high, as our relationship with God is more stable than our feelings. We are not searching for a formula for God to notice us or intervene. We already know his heart is to be with us abundantly. There is freedom in knowing that our participation is in remembering—and even then, we are not called to do that by ourselves.

We have a community among other Christians for that remembrance. Every single discipline brought up in this book has both an individual and communal aspect to it. Even the sacraments have the individual/communal dynamic. An individual receives baptism, one person at a time. But you cannot baptize yourself. You must be baptized by someone outside of you. The same goes for the bread and wine. The elements are going down your individual throat, into your personal stomach. And yet, you are served the element, by someone outside of you. You eat the elements alongside other believers. The spiritual disciplines often follow the pattern set in the sacraments, as God does not ever forget that we are individual persons, and never forgets that we are one body.

However, unlike the sacraments, the spiritual disciplines can be practiced by yourself, and yet you do not have the obligation to do them by yourself. You may pray to God whenever you like. You don't need anyone there for that. But you should also pray for others and with others, and that is your communal aspect. You may read Scripture by yourself, but your reading time is not destroyed if children interrupt, and you start a new habit of reading it aloud to them. Do you use a devotional or commentary someone else in the church wrote? Do you listen to the Scriptures read on audiobook by someone else? Do you hear the Scriptures read in church? Then you are being blessed by the community of saints. In each chapter for each spiritual discipline discussed there will be a portion dedicated to looking at the individual aspect, and a portion dedicated to looking at the communal aspect, as they are linked together.

I know, a definitive "how-to" in the Bible would be easier—or so we think.

- We think if we just had a law, we could keep it. If God would just tell us the particulars of "Love God and love your neighbor" we could do it.
- History has proven otherwise. We cannot keep the law. We can only be kept by Christ.

Safety Is Found in a Person

Several years back we started keeping chickens. When we order chicks, they come packed tightly in a box with holes to the post office.

They can survive 24 hours without food or water, and, knowing the tight time frame, the post office calls us about 5am, sometimes earlier, to let us know that our chicks have arrived at their building. They tell us to come around to the back of the post office and pick them up right away before business hours begin.

Once they're home, we immediately bring the chicks to the brooder. This is a nice, safe environment—a plywood box, with heating lamps, fresh water, and food within easy access. They live there until they become pullets.

Pullets are teenage chickens. They're ugly and awkward. Their downy fuzz has fallen out, but their feathers have only grown in halfway. They aren't laying eggs yet, or if they're roosters, they're not crowing or chasing after hens. They get big, and outgrow their brooder, so eventually we move them up to the chicken coop.

Pullets easily adjust to a new coop. We lock them in there for a few days—a week at most. They get food and water, of course, explore the nesting boxes, and find their favorite perch in their new home. It can be rough on them if there are already older hens in the coop, as they have to work through a new pecking order with all of the new pullets. Eventually, they sort themselves out.

After a few days, we open the doors. All of the older hens rush out and spread across the lawn to search for bugs among the grass, take a bath in the ash pile from our fireplace, or scratch through the compost pile with food scraps. Our yard is a chicken's delight, and by instinct, they return to the coop at night.

The pullets, however, will not leave the coop. They will huddle in a dark corner. They fear the light, they fear the open air, they fear freedom in all of its formS. Freedom does not have walls like the brooder or the coop. The pullets don't care how appealing the yard looks. They don't want to go near anything that could be slightly dangerous. They cannot fathom anything being safe that doesn't look like a barrier.

They haven't met their protector yet.

We have no fences, but we have a livestock guardian dog who is responsible for protecting the chickens. Her name is "Nanny," and as a Great Pyrenees, she takes her job seriously. She will go as far as carrying a pullet by the back of the neck to a better location if it will not move itself. She chases the chickens away from dangerous farm equipment if they get too close. She hunts down and kills predators.

Nanny tends to wander too far in her quest to keep our property predator-free, so when we are not around to keep an eye on things during the day when the chickens are out of the coop, we will tie her up on a long lead by her doghouse in the yard. That way she can keep an eye on the chickens but can't roam too far.

When a coyote, fox, or some other predator comes into our yard, the chickens run towards Nanny. They'll then continue on their search for bugs within the radius of her lead. The older chickens know that if they hunt for bugs within Nanny's radius, she won't let anything touch them. Nanny has pushed chickens into her doghouse, and simply guarded the opening when the predators become too aggressive.

We have to chase the pullets out of the chicken coop aggressively, or they will never leave. We have to teach them that their safety is no longer in the walls; it's in a protector. The pullets cannot know freedom until they learn that. They will waste their lives within the dark four walls of the coop, a place where, if the pullets stay confined for too long, can become full of sickness.

Life in the pasture can be dangerous, but it is also the only place to be free and have literally everything you need. The solution to the danger isn't to run to the "safety" of the coop. The solution is to have a shepherd in the pasture.

Can we accept the fact that God isn't giving us a formula, he's giving us himself?

Sit for a moment and consider what it might look like for you to have God's Holy Spirit with you each and every day, and for that to be enough. Do you dare be curious about a book of the Bible and dive deep—just because you've always wanted to? Are you willing to consider that the spiritual disciplines are less like getting your life organized and more like trying something new, asking God harder questions, and having preconceived ideas of yours be turned upside down as you read God's word? It often doesn't feel organized. In fact, it often feels like you're being uprooted and grafted to a vine with a different life source running through it.

Training Our Response, Not Our Schedule

When we first started homeschooling, I made some enormously detailed spreadsheets itemizing the schedule for each one of my kids. I typed in when I would teach math to each kid. I typed in when the potty-training toddler would have bathroom breaks. I typed in snack time and rotated instrument practice for each kid throughout the day. On paper, I was super organized.

We made it through the first day. I had lost my voice from overshooting the capacity for me to read aloud so much, combined with the constant correction to the kids. I didn't like my kids, and they certainly didn't enjoy me. I figured, we got about 70% of the spreadsheet done! We just have to grow into it! We will get more disciplined over time.

But the interruptions in the days that followed were constant, as was the rebellion in my kids' hearts. The self-righteousness and indignation in my own heart was strong until it crumbled into deep discouragement. *I can't do this homeschool thing. God, you called me wrong.*

A wise, older homeschool mom advised me to throw out the schedule and use a routine in its place. She explained that young kids, toddlers, and babies are much better at routines than schedules. First, we will do this, and then we will do this. Throw out the stopwatch. Teach them to order their days, not try to beat the clock through their days. First breakfast, then reading, then math, then snack. It doesn't matter how long. Just something.

The plan of a routine worked well for five years or so. Then there was a shift in my family, when the older kids were constantly interrupting my teaching time with the younger kids. I kept trying to explain to them that they were stealing my time with their younger brother or sister, and they had to wait their turn. They complained that their turn never came. (Sometimes it didn't . . . usually because they used their time interrupting me 30 times a morning.)

I considered going back to the spreadsheet of a timed schedule to order our days. I wanted the visual for the older kids to see that when they were supposed to be working on one subject independently, my time was blocked off for a different purpose. I wanted them to see that when you take time from one place, you have to cover for it in a different place.

But I remembered my past failings. I remembered the horror of those early spreadsheet days and my arrogance as a fresh homeschooling mom. The routine system worked—until it didn't.

Once again, I talked with a more experienced mom, and she said, "You weren't ready for a schedule system when you had little ones like you did. You've grown into needing something different though. You failed before because it didn't fit your life then. Your life is different now. Your family has different needs."

So, I typed out, printed, and laminated new schedules for our kitchen bulletin board. This was their class schedule. If the older ones took my time out of turn, they had to find a way, later in their schedule, to restore that time. They could still interrupt me for emergencies, heartbreaks, or unusual situations. The problem had been the "Hey mom, did you know that a lobster . . ." interruptions.

The new system worked. It was the visual the older kids needed so that finally my younger kids had the time they needed with me to get their schoolwork done.

Which system was best?

As we put spiritual disciplines into a liturgical "system" of our days, we must keep our unique needs in mind. While the law is inflexible, fulfilled only by Christ, liturgy is incredibly flexible and changeable as it is God's gift *for you*. It is for our support. It trains us to depend on the works of Christ, by training us to respond to the Holy Spirit who is always pointing us to Christ. Schedules can respond to a need, but they are not the goal. Responding to the Holy Spirit's leading to fix our gaze on Christ is the goal.

There are seasons when reading my Bible is first thing in the morning. There are seasons when I need a new habit like staying off the phone and screens during certain hours, setting aside time to pray for even five or ten minutes, or having a Bible reading plan. It is also true that many people have these habits, and their hearts are far from God.

If excellent spiritual habits made you a super Christian, then the Judaizers of the New Testament would have been super Christians. They were the most disciplined, the ones displaying the law best. They were willing to carve off the nerves most sensitive on their bodies, and the bodies of their sons. They had the ritual of prayer, and the rituals of the sabbath. They held strictly to diets and laws for their bodies.

If you read the apostle Paul for even a few verses in his many books, he never once says these rituals should be avoided. He said they don't matter. Do them. Don't do them. It's Jesus who saves you.

The Holy Spirit is gentle, but persistent. In order to show us the sufficiency of Christ, he will repeatedly expose our insufficiency, therefore hiding our weakness is counterproductive. His leading may look like a melting of the heart towards an issue. Your heart will start to crave Scripture or prayer. Your mind might be unsettled, or there is a situation you cannot get out of your mind—a neighbor who needs help, a parent who needs honor, a child who needs an apology. His leading often feels like an awareness to an unsettling within us, as he is guiding us to a place of peace.

"The Holy Spirit is no Skeptic, and it is not doubts or mere opinions that he has written on our hearts, but assertions more sure and certain than life itself and all experience."[1]

God's Spirit lives in us, and while he is a Comforter, he also uproots us more often than we would like as a means to root out false comforts. I have found that, when I yield to this calling, when I scratch the itch he starts, or even be brave enough to wrestle with God, he meets me there. When I pray to him even though I'm angry, even though I'm frustrated, even though I feel like I have barely a drop of faith, I lay my heart bare, and I dare him to show me what he's trying to get through to me—that's when he grows me.

Obedience doesn't gain favor with my father as much as it gives me a greater understanding of his love—his repetitive, unending, unstoppable love.

It's vital that we talk about the "why" of obedience. If we simply say God demands our obedience and fail to contextualize that fact within the truth of the gospel, we are being dangerously reckless with the use of Scripture. It's not that obeying God is bad, quite the opposite. The gospel does not change what is right and wrong. But proclaiming that all God wants from us is obedience without pointing to the sufficient obedience of Christ isn't just inching towards heresy, it's longing for salvation by ourselves through God's "advice."

We must remember that God freely interrupts our plans, therefore, it would be imprudent to make carefully laid plans our ultimate goal. Having a perfectly kept schedule usually requires us to limit "messy people" from our lives, and God has called us to go to them. Needy people will persistently mess up our schedules and routines. Focusing on our plans, rather than understanding the purpose of the plans is like seeing the beauty of creation and worshiping it rather than the Creator. Putting spiritual disciplines into the liturgies of our lives trains us as responders, not as perfect, untouched routine keepers.

We must anticipate that God will interrupt our schedules as he trains us to respond. One of my old mentors used to say that when she woke up every day, she would look at her to-do list, and pray that as the day progressed, God would add to the list what she had missed, and would take things off the list that weren't meant for her. Then she would start her day, welcoming interruptions as God's correction of her plans.

We cannot find perfection in a schedule or routines. Liturgies are there to serve us, with a deep understanding of our human needs. The Holy Spirit will train us in our responses to the struggles of this life, and he won't leave us without resources to know him abundantly. We can only find freedom through dependence on him—dependence on anything else is slavery.

CHAPTER 7

Rest

"And yet no leaf or grain is filled
By work of ours; the field is tilled
And left to grace. That we may reap,
Great work is done while we're asleep."

—WENDELL BERRY[1]

YOU MAY BE TEMPTED to approach this section of the book with pen, paper, and a drive to try to master each new discipline.

Let's get on with this! It's about Christ—got it. Now what do we *do*?

Well, let's start with nothing. It's harder than it sounds. What kind of control freaks are we humans that we need a whole chapter, or even shelves of books, teaching us how to rest? We so often want a how-to for everything—even how to do nothing.

For instance, my husband and I both have different methods of sleeping. I'm a night owl, and I have a specific routine to get myself to sleep, otherwise I end up lying down, not sleeping for hours. Insomnia and I are close friends. My husband, on the other hand, shakes his head at my strict list of "how to get to sleep." He says, "This is how I fall asleep: step one, lie down. There is no step two."

The call to rest is neither theoretical nor merely practical. It's not just physical, just spiritual, or some other fraction of ourselves. It's comprehensive. God has given us—our whole selves—rest. We don't have to complete rest, earn rest, or achieve rest.

"Come ye all who are weary and heavy laden, and I will give you rest," Jesus says in Matthew 11:28. Rest feels illusive. It often feels just out of reach. How do we obtain it? Emily P. Freeman reflects on sitting under the teaching of A.J. Swoboda,

> He mentions that no where in the Bible are we asked to create or make Sabbath. Instead, we protect it and enter into it. It's not something we make up, it's something we've been asked to take care of. He points out how the Jews knew this and they spoke of *keeping* Sabbath, not creating it. They would understand the difference. It isn't something they decided to do because they were really tired and needed a break. No, Sabbath is a gift, and they were wise to receive it.[2]

We are not the creators of rest. We are the receivers.

So then, how do we receive the gift of rest in our daily lives? How do we keep it? How does a nursing mother experience a sabbath? Does she stop nursing for the day? Families can't stop eating one day a week. Breaking up fights can't stop one day a week. Dishes pile up seven days out of seven. Weeds still grow on the weekend. Resting would be so much easier if the needs of life would stop one day a week. The needs of this life growl at us day after day with little regard for our fatigue.

Our human penchant for pragmatism fuels our resistance to Jesus' invitation to rest. No matter how hard we may try, we can't think ourselves out of our gut-level opposition to the spirit of sabbath.

Unable to resolve our dissonance, we often set out to seek our comfort instead of true rest. If that sounds conflicting, consider if some of the following statements sound familiar to you.

- "I just can't relax until the dishes are washed up"?
- "This is just going to bother me unless I finish it quickly."

We describe work as an itch that we must scratch in order to rest. Let's finish up all of our work first. Then we will rest.

But the work doesn't stop. It continues to pop up like weeds in the garden. Unable to break the cycle, we seek after the temporary comfort of completing at least a portion of our work in order to experience rest. We cringe at the idea of any work being done *for us* so that we can rest.

"That's not rest." We say. "That's laziness." We don't rest when there's work to be done. Of course, work is not bad for us. We would do well to recognize it is also from God. Like the relationship between law and gospel, work gives meaning to the value of rest. Rest is deeper when we have worked hard. In the Old Testament, people worked for 6 days, and *after* that, they rested. Likewise, if we do not know our sin, if the full weight of the law has not been understood or even attempted, we don't understand the destruction from which we were forgiven. The weight of the law helps us understand the gospel. The action of work helps us understand rest. Work is not evil, unless it twists out of place in God's divine order.

Resting on Resurrection Sunday

After Jesus' death and resurrection, God's people began to celebrate the sabbath on Sunday. The simple reason for that is because the resurrection was on Sunday, but the detailed version of this reason is much more fun.

Justin Martyr, a mid-second-century theologian, wrote about how the early church moved to observing the sabbath on Saturday to Sunday. The first day of the week, in biblical terms, is the first day of creation, or the first dawning of a new world, Justin explained.[3] In Genesis 1, this was the day when the Godhead proclaimed, "Let there be light." When the week was complete on day seven, God rested.

The church fathers first discussed the idea of an "eighth day" of creation in terms of God's covenant with Abraham given through the sign of circumcision in Genesis 17. Some refer to Resurrection Sunday as the "eighth day" of creation, which Justin Martyr paralleled with the practice of circumcision on the eighth day of a boy's life. Israel believed that circumcision was a sign, or a promise of new life—restored, redeemed life—on the eighth day.

In church liturgy, Holy Week walks through purposeful, intentional signs and prophecies fulfilled leading up to the crucifixion. If we are to parallel God's week of creation and Jesus' Holy Week, the day that God created man in creation (Friday) is the day Jesus was tortured and died on the cross. The day that God rested (Saturday) is the day Jesus lay still in the tomb. The church tradition of Holy Week, the week leading up to Easter, is celebrated from Sunday to Saturday. Then on the eighth day, Resurrection Sunday—new life.

Justin argued that the sabbath was not even kept by the Israelites or Moses and was only given as a sign to Israel and a temporary measure because of Israel's sinfulness, no longer needed after Christ came without sin.[4] As much as they tried, Israel could not keep the sabbath perfectly. It wasn't given for their perfection. It was given as a sign to them. Not as individuals, and not as a community. The plan was never for them to be saved through the law. God didn't give the law to save the people, but to direct them to his final salvation. Therefore, the eighth day is a celebration of our eternal sabbath in Christ. It's not a day, it's a life—a resurrected life.

A resurrected life begins with rest. It contemplates how we received this rest and, how we can possibly deserve this rest we did not earn. Anything we do for the remainder of the week springs forth from the starting point of rest.

Justin Martyr argues that one of the reasons we cannot believe in righteousness through circumcision (the law), is that only men are circumcised.[5] Don't miss the significance of this. If circumcision saved us, as the Judaizers believed, then only men would be saved. The eighth day, however, is a gift, a completion of the promise of which circumcision was a reminder, the promise of new life and eternal rest—given to both male and female.

Consider:

- If righteousness comes through circumcision, then how do women obtain it?
- If righteousness comes through rising early to pray, then how do people who work nights obtain it?
- If righteousness comes through reading through the Bible fully every year, then how do Christians who don't have access to a full Bible at home, and only hear the word at church services obtain it?
- If righteousness comes through a consistent schedule of devotions, then how do mothers with a colicky baby obtain it?

That's the thing about any works-based salvation (justification or sanctification) plan. When we filter a "rich spiritual life" through a cultural lens, whether that be white, middle class, stay-at-home mom, 9-to-5 job, American/Western realities, etc., we will develop a list of things people in that bracket are able to do, and make that "the law" that brings forth life within them. We forget two fundamental truths when we apply cultural filters. First, God didn't give laws that specific. Second, life doesn't come through the law, it comes through the gospel (Gal. 2:20–21). Life comes when the Holy Spirit breathes new life into something that was dead.

What about the mother in Africa, who spends her entire day finding and preparing food for her family? Where is her spirituality? Where is her righteousness? What about the slave in a sweatshop? What about the mentally disabled? What about those who lack the capacity, in either time, resources, accessibility, or physical ability?

Works-based righteousness favors the able-bodied, the talented, and the rich. Works-based righteousness has favorites.

When one of these lists of how to achieve righteousness is developed and adopted with only the worldly elites in mind, danger ensues. On the surface, the list isn't a problem for the able, the talented, and the rich to accomplish. However, when they make themselves a list of the "important laws" and then meet their own expectations, they forget their need for a Savior. They have effectively removed Jesus from the equation. They form a checklist: check, check, check. "I'm good."

One example of this in Scripture is found in Mark 10:17–27.

> "And as he was setting out on his journey, a man ran up and knelt before him and asked him, 'Good Teacher, what must I do to inherit eternal life?' And Jesus said to him, 'Why do you call me good? No one is good except God alone. You know the commandments: "Do not murder, Do not commit adultery, Do not steal, Do not bear false witness, Do not defraud, Honor your father and mother."' And he said to him, 'Teacher, all these I have kept from my youth.' And Jesus, looking at him, loved him, and said to him, 'You lack one thing: go, and sell all you have and

give to the poor, and you will have treasure in heaven; and come, follow me.' Disheartened by the saying, he went away sorrowful, for he had great possessions. And Jesus looked around and said to his disciples, 'How difficult it will be for those who have wealth to enter the kingdom of God!' And the disciples were amazed at his words. But Jesus said to them again, 'Children, how difficult it is to enter the kingdom of God! It is easier for a camel to go through the eye of an needle than for a rich person to enter the kingdom of God.' And they were exceedingly astonished, and said to him, 'Then who can be saved?' Jesus looked at them and said, 'With man it is impossible, but not with God. For all things are possible with God.'"

That poor, rich man. He thought his good works would impress God himself. God in the flesh essentially told him, (to paraphrase) "First off, you're not as good as you think you are. Only God is good. I don't need these good works, but your neighbors do. Give your good works—pour them out on those who need it, and follow me, who can actually give you eternal life." Our money is often the biggest representation of our work that we have. Jesus told him to give his riches to the poor.

Our righteousness comes from Christ. Our good works are for our neighbors; they are not presented to God in exchange for love. We are already approved on account of Christ, not our works.

It's not insignificant that the liturgy of Sunday worship was developed early on in the church, to remind us that while God has prepared good works for us to do, we walk into them from a place of resting in the resurrection.

Righteousness comes through faith in Christ who was crucified for sinners. He wasn't crucified for the capable. In fact, he kept trying to explain to the Pharisees that able-ness is an illusion that is dangerous.

In Christ, we are overcomers (1 John 4:4). But our works come out of Christ's righteousness, and while he gives us gifts to bless our neighbors with an outpouring of his love, he seems to especially like to overcome areas that we consider dead and hopeless. He does bring discipline to the undisciplined (Heb. 12:6). He is the father to the fatherless.

This is a beautiful fulfillment of God's covenant to have the resurrection on the eighth day. Circumcision was a sign that a messiah would come, most bluntly put and most vividly portrayed, through the offspring of the circumcised.

God commanded the Israelites to perform the sign of circumcision on the eighth day. Why? Babies begin to produce Vitamin K on the eighth day after birth. Vitamin K contributes to blood clotting, so it's dangerous to circumcise earlier. Early theologians didn't have access to that scientific knowledge, but they did know that the eighth day was a sign of a new life—a life rooted in promise, given to someone who hasn't done anything.

We should remember that rest and worship are neither required nor limited to any day of the week now. The early church gifted us with a liturgy to point us to the fulfillment of the promise, but not as a new law. The new law is written on our hearts, by the Holy Spirit who speaks in Scripture, and points to Christ. We are free because we are not boxed in by rules. Instead, we are guided and protected by a person.

We are not excluded from any of this because we are female, or because we have a harder life than some. Consider the command given to Moses, the law that Christ completely fulfilled: "Remember the Sabbath day, to keep it holy. Six days you shall labor, and do all your work, but the seventh day is a Sabbath to the Lord your God. On it you shall not do any work, you, or your son, or your daughter,yourmaleservant,oryourfemaleservant,oryourlivestock,or the sojourner who is within your gates." (Exod. 20:8–10).

When Christ came to bring rest to his people, when he fulfilled the law, he didn't restrict regular rest to men or women, son or daughter, master or servant—even the homeless with nothing were not left out.

It is impossible to grasp the richness of the gospel if we cannot put down our work. Therefore, when we share the gospel with others, we need to remember that they cannot hear us if we do not provide a way for them to put down their work. When we want to encourage others with the grace of God, it will often start by looking for ways to help them rest.

A New Testament sabbath isn't work, then rest. It's Day 1: rest, because your work is completed in Christ first and foremost. This does not mean that God has not graciously given us good works to do but that we start from a place of remembering what Christ has done on our behalf. Everything we do comes out of our rest found in Christ, not moving towards our rest in Christ.

Our Perfect Design

Our need for rest is not a flaw, but part of our original, perfect design. God created us to need rest one day per week, which we know because he revealed the pattern of work and rest in Genesis 1 and 2. The fall doesn't occur until Genesis 3, so growing tired isn't a byproduct of the fall.

God designed us to need rest that way for a purpose—so that we take the time to see him at work. It's a regular time when we face the fact that the world does not rest on our own shoulders. Throwing rest out the door is contrary to nature, contrary to how God made us, and contrary to what God has called good. Why is that? It might seem God is overemphasizing the power of a good nap.

When Jesus completed the law, he became our love of God, and he became our love of neighbor. He became our satisfaction. He became our faithfulness. He became our rest.

When we talk about "rest," we should clarify if we mean physical rest or spiritual rest. The answer here is: both. Only the Gnostic heretics believed that God cared only about the spiritual. God has chosen these bodies for us and designed these bodies for us. They are limited, as part of their design. Our limitations are "good." Rest is still *for us*. Rest is still necessary *for us*. Our design is unchanged. It is still good.

We no longer define rest by rules like not using scissors on the sabbath, not walking more than 1/4 mile, or other defining terms that the legalists used to rate how well they were resting as a means of impressing God. We do not fulfill a promise. We submit to a Spirit that is *for us*. We find our physical and spiritual rest in a person.

Though the early church writings refer to worshipping on Sunday, we are not ever told in the Bible to rest exactly on Sunday. The new covenant does not command us to fulfill a set of rules. The idea of rest in the new covenant should permeate every part of our lives. We fix our eyes on the principles of freedom and loving our neighbors. We can, theoretically, pick any day of the week to rest. Those who work in hospitals and patrol streets on Sundays are not any less spiritual for celebrating rest on a different day of the week.

Now that we know why the early church started their week with rest, why do we begin with rest in this book of disciplines? Our Sunday worship usually includes both word and sacrament, so reading God's word is not excluded from this day of rest. This is not intended to be any sort of ranking, but it should make you wonder—why does the discipline of nothing, or stillness, need to be discussed before the discipline of action?

Rest feeds into Bible study, empowers us to pray, sets the foundation for meditation. Before God shows us something, he often calls us to stop doing what we are doing.

God is not primarily concerned if you pull weeds on Sunday. He is concerned with the heart issue that drives you to keep working as though the world depended on you. Remember the root sin from the Garden of Eden? It wasn't enough for Adam and Eve to be near God, to be with God, to be godly. No, they wanted to throw off their limitations and be "like God." We want to be accomplished to continually get ahead, and no one has ever won a resting award.

I asked the question once: is rest considered law or gospel? We might say that it depends if rest is a command or a gift. What we mean by that is: is rest optional? Obviously, it's part of the 10 commandments. "Remember the Sabbath day, to keep it holy. Six days you shall labor, and do all your work, but the seventh day is a Sabbath to the LORD your God. On it you shall not do any work, you, or your son, or your daughter, your male servant, or your female servant, or your livestock, or the sojourner who is within your gates" (Exod. 20:8–10).

God took his people's lack of rest very seriously. He commanded rest not just for the individual but for a people. Rest was a sign of justice—it ensured that, making sure everyone, regardless of age, gender, or station, received it. And yet, Jesus said that man wasn't made for the sabbath, but the sabbath was made for man (Mark 2:27). God built rest into creation and confirmed its importance when giving the 10 Commandments. The book of Hebrews associates rest with belief and grace as part of the new covenant. Rest is for us. God gives us a gift of doing nothing as we sit and just receive. The very idea drips with the gospel.

It is finished.

The Rest-Faith Connection

Hebrews 3–4 relates rest with belief, not with work, preparation, or timing. "Rest" is another word for the promised land, or the land to which the Israelites entered from Egypt. Egypt represents slavery. The promised land represents rest.

With any work project, whether farming, writing, or whatever your vocation, we can build up a sort of momentum where things are getting done, we feel like we are moving forward, and the last thing that we want to do is stop and lose any ground that we have gained. And yet, that is what God asks us to do—for our good.

The beautiful gift of rest is that it recalibrates us to the truth of *who* truly accomplishes tasks. This realization does not deter our overall production, but typically increases it for the simple reason—that God accomplishes more than we can. God works in and through us all the time, but to pause and *watch him work* is an act of worship. Beholding God at work draws us into worship, into simply naming the works of his hands.

The more I practice rest, the more I laugh at the idea that simply watching God at work could somehow reduce production. His work is the only work that matters. Resting points to our need for God. This is most apparent to me when I am trying to teach my children. I will talk, and lecture, and give examples, and try to get them to understand a truth that they don't like on the surface. But then I stop, and pray, "Lord, show them what I cannot," and I lay down the burden of

· 92 ·

convincing them in my way, on my timetable, God will soften their hearts to joyfully embrace that same truth in ways my rhetoric couldn't reach them. Some days I think he has me stop and watch, so that I can lay down the burden, and remember he is the one in control.

So, rest. Sketch a flower in bloom. Lie in the grass and study the clouds, drifting by overhead, like watching the underbellies of whales drift by in the currents. How could we think the world stops when we stop? How amazing is it that God gives little ones like us good work to do? What kind of love is this that doesn't set our value and worth based on what we can produce?

Rest is the practice of acknowledging our limitations—which is humbling, because if we ignore our limitations, we can continue believing we are like God, instead of created by God. We need to call our need for rest "good." This consistent humbling roots us in our identity as humans, not gods. We are humans in need of God, not self-sufficient co-gods alongside Christ. Knowing our place and our relationship to God roots our bodies in truth.

The Rest-Community Connection

My mom worked for a Christian relief and community development non-profit for some decades. Her work taught me that it's hard for a person struggling with thirst to hear the gospel. Our physical needs and spiritual needs are not as separate as we might imagine. They are tangled together, as God often uses our bodies to illustrate to us spiritual truths. We don't baptize a person's spirit; we baptize their body. Communion is physically consumed, not theoretically imagined.

The gospel doesn't ignore the real, practical concerns of the body. In other words, the spiritual disciplines do not assert the superiority of the spiritual over the physical. The Gnostic heretics in the early church were famous for considering anything physical or material, not just as unimportant, but as evil.

How often are we so overcome with guilt that we have trouble spending time reading our Bibles? We've barely slept in days. We try to claim our identities as faithful ones who do not give up routines easily. We despise the limitations on our bodies that God has given us, so we press on, shaming ourselves along the way when we can't focus or stay awake, when we hunger and thirst.

The needs of our bodies are not evil; they are part of what God called "good" in all of creation.

The need to rest—the need to be ministered to by someone outside of us—is good.

Resting is the practice of *not* producing. In a culture that finds its identity in how much it produces, rest provides a weekly reset. The spirit of this discipline is for God to slow us down enough to notice what he is producing. When rest is skipped, anxiety and stress skyrocket, as we start to believe that everything depends on us. The world cannot go on without our work, we think. Without realizing it, we appoint ourselves the saviors of our own little worlds. Forcing ourselves to rest means that we are admitting that the world will go on without us. The sun will keep rising and setting. Things will get done—though often not the way we would manage them.

Rest is most difficult for the control freaks among us, who find more joy in neatly ordering the world to their standards than in learning to sit in the mess and the patience of it all. Rest is for our good, but that doesn't mean it's comfortable.

> "Rest is synonymous with grace, which is never seized by force, but always taken hold of freely by faith. Rest is also synonymous with Christ, who is both its primary proponent and

chief architect. The first step in the radical pursuit of rest is to seek Christ. This is also the last step. When you find Christ, you will find rest."[6]

There have been times in my life when rest was simply not possible outside of community. When people bring meals when my family is sick, it gives me a moment to rest instead of cook. When people who love my children well care for them while I am at Bible study, I grow in my faith. Some seasons sabbath after sabbath gets sabotaged by life, and I have to reach out to someone and say, "Help. I don't know how to get through this." I still struggle with the shame of that—the shame of needing others. However, just like God gives us forgiveness, and we should then give forgiveness to others. God gives us rest, and we should give others rest, too.

Where We Go from Here

The only "work" involved in rest, is to make sure that our neighbors are able to rest as well. Like the gospel, we cannot forget those who cannot. Since we have no specifications on how we should practice rest, we should assume two things: First, rest is Spirit-led. Second, our practices of rest will vary by circumstance.

Things we do know from Scripture: rest is communal. We must make sure everyone gets it. We must notice who needs rest. We must speak up when we are personally not getting rest. We also see in Scripture that God intends us to practice rest regularly. A weekly observance is good, but there are seasons when more or less times of rest can logistically happen. Jesus calls us to remember that rest is for us, not above or against us.

The Holy Spirit must help you develop ideas for rest and draw your attention to areas in your life where rest is needed. You may not have the challenges of marriage or children, but you have your own unique situation that will require rest. In my household, my husband naps every Sunday afternoon. The rest of us take a daily "quiet time" that started with the little ones' nap and became almost a "siesta" time after lunch where, during our homeschool, we just stop and take a breather, and little ones can nap. Since we have eight people in our household, and no dishwasher, dishes take up a huge portion of my life, as does any food preparation. We have multiple food allergies in our home, so I often cook food from scratch, which takes a lot of dishes, time, and attention to cleanliness. So, on Sundays, we usually eat on paper plates and eat prepackaged, or not-prepared-by-me, food. Just cutting those tasks out of my Sundays allows me to rest—to go for a walk, stare out the window, and reflect on the works of God in my family's life.

Whenever I go for weeks on end without rest, my productivity decreases. I slow to a dragging pace. I lose my temper on everyone, and the Spirit points me to my need for rest, my need for grace. My physical need for rest reminds me of my spiritual need for grace.

In moments like these, it's critical that I pray for wisdom, and not just assume that what seems practical is automatically what is wise. The wisdom of rest often involves humbly asking for help. It often involves generously offering to help. Much like the entire Christian life, God did not design the discipline of rest to be practiced in isolation. The goal isn't perfection. The goal is rest.

CHAPTER 8

Bible Reading

"I did nothing. The Word did everything"

—MARTIN LUTHER[1]

SATAN WILL CALL YOU a "legalist" when you try to regularly pray and read your Bible. Then he will call you a "failure" when you forget to do those things. Remember, we will never satisfy Satan, because the fact is, he doesn't get to name us, and the One who does name us is satisfied already on account of Christ.

There is likely no other discipline that will make you feel categorized or rated as a Christian than Bible reading. We humans have made extra rules about it all. We ask questions like: when is the holiest time of day to read the Bible? Should you read a chapter a day, or is it better to read through the Bible in the year? Does it "count" to read a devotional that walks you through just one verse? If you don't understand a passage, should you just keep trudging through? Is it wrong to use the word "trudge" for Bible reading?

Most of these questions arise in response to verses like Romans 10:17, "So faith comes from hearing, and hearing through the word of Christ." Faith comes through hearing the word of Christ. Therefore, if you want more faith, get more of the word. With an equation that simple, we should hold nothing back and just study the Bible night and day. What's stopping us at 30 minutes a day? Why not four hours? We think this way because we still believe that our works will give us an edge on faith. If reading the Bible is a "work" and a lot of "works" give us more faith, then let's do them a lot! But the faith God wants to grow in us is not faith in our abilities, but it's faith in Christ's.

Before we talk about reading God's word, let's examine the emotional baggage we have associated with it, so that we can recognize what we needlessly attach to this gift.

- Do you feel guilty when you miss a day of Bible reading?
- Do you feel shame for how much you dread reading the Bible?
- Do you have to bribe yourself to read the Bible?
- Do you feel the need to keep pushing to the end of the chapter, even when you have a question in the middle?
- When you don't understand the Bible, does it shake your faith?
- Are you intimidated by reading the Bible on its own, without a devotional, like you're not smart enough to understand it?
- Do you feel guilty if you don't get much out of your Bible reading time?
- Have you ever listed Bible reading as a New Year's resolution, and made it until Numbers?
- Does it count?
- Was it enough?
- What if I don't understand?
- What am I getting out of it anyway?

We bring a lot of baggage to our Bible reading, and that baggage can have theological implications as we approach God's word.

Hermeneutic practices matter. Reading within a community—hearing the word preached—matters. God gave us the Bible as a gift. It's not a noose around our necks. However, because we form to it, not it to us, we often wrestle with it as it challenges and shapes us. It will make us uncomfortable at times. But if the Bible is the Holy Spirit's vocabulary, then knowing it is essential to hearing his voice.

Individual "Quiet Time"

The actual practice of quiet time (sitting and reading your Bible on your own) is good, but internalizing it as an expectation can trigger attacks in your deepest self, down to your very assurance of salvation. When the perfect quiet time wasn't available to me due to "seasons" with little kids, I went through self-pity, self-loathing, blaming kids, blaming my body or fatigue, and blaming my community. Though I felt a lot of things, I wasn't bringing these emotions of anger and hatred to God. I needed to ask God to make a way, but I felt it was my responsibility to make a way, not his. Bible reading was supposed to be my act of worship, my part of the faith equation, and I was terrible at it. I didn't want to face the fact that I wasn't that great at having devotions even before I had kids. It was easier to blame my circumstances and be the martyr instead of asking for help.

In my desire to be more consistently in God's word, I listened to many Bible teachers. They would use the law to say things like "you can't read a little 1-verse devotional a day and call yourself a Christian" and "the reason you don't read your Bible every day is that you don't want it badly enough. You don't prioritize it enough. It's your desire that's the problem that needs fixing."

Obviously. I agree my heart is the problem. I need help with my heart. That *is* the problem. How do I fix it? How do I want it more? How do I prioritize correctly? What do I do to get myself to read my Bible?

The solution to your heart is to read your Bible, they say. Just buck up and do it. This is a cyclical argument that does not require community involvement except perhaps in the form of accountability partners who will "call you out" and try to convict you if you fail. These claims come with a lot of the baggage of individual, accomplished spirituality.

If you struggle to regularly read your Bible, the only way to resolve that in your heart is to "hear the Word." Romans 10:14–17 says "How then will they call on him in whom they have not believed? And how are they to believe in him of whom they have not heard? And how are they to hear without someone preaching? And how are they to preach unless they are sent? As it is written 'How beautiful are the feet of those who preach the good news!' For Isaiah says, 'Lord, who has believed what he has heard from us?' So faith comes from hearing, and hearing through the word of Christ."

Notice Paul says, "hear the word" not "read the word." Look at the community involvement in that text. Will there be a time in your Christian life where you will ever *not* need to hear that Jesus is carrying you, he is the faithful one, he died for your sins? As Christians, we love to take that last part and turn it into a law that says, "if you want to grow your faith, then you need to read the Bible regularly." That interpretation ignores the context. It ignores that Romans says that your faith grows when someone preaches the word of Christ to us. It forgets that when someone points you to Scripture and all that Christ has done from the very beginning, your faith is rooted.

Think about the number of years the common people in church did not have access to reading a Bible daily, but only had access to the Scripture through hearing it. How can we hear the word outside community—outside someone speaking the word to us?

Perhaps some people find it helpful to grit their teeth and push through to read what they don't desire to read or struggle to understand. "So is my word that goes out from my mouth: It will not return to me empty, but will accomplish what I desire and achieve the purpose for which I sent it." Isaiah 55:11 is often said to point out that fact. This sometimes works, but it often leaves us with the belief that it is all up to us as individuals, that we each have to push through, that the strength of our faith is on our shoulders, and we just need to develop it like a potter to the clay.

Has it occurred to us that we are to be in the word of God not just to develop our own faith, but for the purpose of encouraging those around us with the message of the gospel, both in and out of church? I have to admit, I want to be the most knowledgeable, the most respectable, the wisest person in my circle.

We have to ask ourselves—when we approach our Bible reading, do we push through because we want to be the disciple Jesus loves the most and sit at his right hand? Perhaps there's a reason we fail often at it.

Growing in Humility

Developing daily habits of Bible reading starts with the admission that we are horrible at it. We have to understand that the solution to our lack is God—every—single—time. I prayed an embarrassing prayer several years back. I was frustrated and ashamed of my lack of consistency. I asked God that he would make me crave his word more than I craved coffee in the morning. *I asked him to change my heart and give me the follow through.* How idolatrous can I be that I value my coffee everyday more than I value God's word? No one confesses that out loud. What I learned through that prayer is that God always loves answering that prayer. He loves the humble cry of his child that says "fix my heart, because it isn't doing what it should do! Help me crave the right things! Make me so uncomfortable without your word that I cannot be comfortable or settled without it!"

We don't often pray for God to make us uncomfortable each day until we are satisfied in absorbing Scripture, mostly because we know he answers those kinds of prayers. We are less sure if he will answer prayers about our comfort, or money, or health. We pray those kinds of prayers and assume that God will say yes or no depending on his wisdom. But prayers asking to be made uncomfortable for his purpose—we know he will answer those. And this creates a problem for us because we don't want God to take any drastic steps. We want to ease ourselves in. We want spiritual growth to happen on our terms and schedules. It's not that we don't think the Holy Spirit can himself daily draw us to his word. It's that we don't trust his methods, which are extraordinarily effective.

Honestly, it's not that I don't like Bible reading plans, checklists, or resolutions. Those are useful, neutral tools. It's that I don't trust my human heart to see them through—and even if it can see them through, I don't trust my human heart to give God the glory for that achievement.

We must get it through our heads that the Holy Spirit is always reliable to change our hearts. He is the dependable one, not us. He's not an unreliable wisp, moving in and out of our lives. Neither is he a tyrant, being brutal in his love. This is the Spirit of Christ himself, who laid down his life for us. His Spirit is given *for us* and Jesus promised he will be *with us* and he is a thousand times more reliable to hold us to his word than our own hearts are. Ask him to give you the craving, and just see what he will do.

Modern Ideas of Devotions

As the Holy Spirit worked on the cravings of my heart, my eyes became increasingly aware of how individualistic I saw my Bible reading goals. "Devotions" or "quiet time" are the buzzwords of the second half of the twentieth century. Personal Bible time became a focus among Evangelicals. These are not bad terms, but it should be noted that they are new ones. Nineteen hundred years of church history didn't include those words, and you won't find them mentioned in the Bible.

Bonhoeffer speaks about the importance of individual time with God. He says that seeking just an individual faith experience is just as dangerous as seeking only communal experiences. "One who wants fellowship without solitude plunges into the void of words and feelings, and one who seeks solitude without fellowship perishes in the abyss of vanity, self-infatuation and despair."[2]

A holistic faith will be both individual and communal. God sees our individual hearts. God has placed us within communities. When we rely on only our gatherings for an intake of God's word, we will be subject to consider our faith through the lenses of experience, feelings about experiences, and atmosphere. When we rely only on our personal readings of Scripture, we will soon become full of ourselves and our own intellectual understandings.

We also run the risk of massively intaking the word of God, but not letting the effects of it pour out on our neighbors. If we aren't teaching, whether it's the little ones in our homes, our neighbors all around us, a Sunday school class, or even letting the weight of the word affect our actions, we read only for ourselves. We too often read to puff ourselves up. In Bible school, some of my professors had a joking, and crude, phrase for this phenomenon: spiritual constipation.

Church history is a story of swinging pendulums, of ideas that were responses to other ideas. These movements in history attempted to reorient whatever the church culture was at that time to what was true. Heresies were revealed, and they reappeared when the pendulum swung back in the prior direction.

The pendulum between corporate and individual emphasis when it comes to relationship with God continues to swing. We must remember—we're always called to both. God sees us as individuals. God sees us as his one bride. We do not have a relationship with God in isolation from the rest of his church. It is never "just me and Jesus." No matter how often you meet with other believers, if you belong to Christ, you belong to his one body. If we hold to the mystery of the Trinity, we must also accept the mystery of church unity. We are one body.

All of this is built upon the truth that God's word is living and active in our lives. But what does that mean? When I have mourned that my role as a caregiver often means I can't access uninterrupted routines, God has taught me to delight in the flexibility and freedom of getting his word in me—which usually involves hearing God's word within a community. I can listen to a sermon on his word—when a pastor gives me the word of God and explains it to me. I can read his word by myself. I can memorize his word. I can listen to someone read the word as an audiobook while I'm driving. I can listen to it as I exercise. I can read it aloud to my children.

God does not specify the "how" because he knows that any mandated "how" will be turned into law, and faith does not come through the letter of the law, it comes through the word of Christ—the completion of the law. Faith does not come from doing the right things. Faith comes from the Holy Spirit who continually points us to Christ, through his word.

As noted in the chapter on rest, when we make righteousness about our works, we immediately show favoritism for those who are capable in the eyes of the world. The flexibility and diverse nature of the how and when and how much isn't just pragmatic—it's at the very core of walking by the Spirit, instead of walking by the law (Gal. 5:18).

I have always been struck by the fact that Corrie Ten Boom's family, a family that took in and hid Jews during the Holocaust, read from the Bible together each morning. The grandfather would read it, and whichever neighbors were by would stay and listen. He would just read it. No devotional was prepared. He did this so often that they were all fed regularly.

When Corrie and her sister were sent to the Ravensbrück concentration camp, and they were able to miraculously smuggle in a Bible, they simply read it and talked about it. The words had worn so familiar that they were able to meditate on Scripture when the book was not open or available. When routine helped them, they used routine. When routine was not possible, God's word remained in them and with them. The Holy Spirit did not come and go as their lives turned upside down. Their routines did not harm them, but their faith did not decrease as their routines fell away.

It's hard for me to write that because I'm an introvert and a perfectionist, and my personality loves alone *anything*. I love reading my Bible alone, praying alone, going for walks alone. My day is full of many children and so many interruptions, that my thoughts begin to stutter inside my head.

May we learn first to receive from a place of passive rest. From that place of being filled to the measure, being hearers of the word, we can then go live in that extravagant love. What does that mean? It means that we live in the remembrance that we have full access to God—so much access to love that we can take as much as we want and pour it on our neighbors.

Communal Bible Reading

Every church, whether casual or formal, has a liturgy. It is the order of the service, as often printed in a bulletin. The liturgy may play out like this—we hear the Scripture being read—often one passage from the Old Testament and one from the New Testament. We sing hymns and songs of praise. Then we hear the word of God preached by a pastor who takes the word of God, reads it, then explains it. Depending on the church's customs, we then receive communion, as we are called to remember, through tangible, sensory means, that Jesus was given for us.

A church service is about one of the most beautiful ways to start the week from a place of rest and *receive* what God has for you. God's word is spoken over us. Jesus' body, called "The Word" is given to us to hold and consume, to remind us that this isn't just theoretical. What he is offering us is tangible, practical, supernatural, and we do not produce in this service—we consume. We are gifted. We are individuals participating as one body, through grace.

Being Discipled

We are discipled in Scripture at church. If we only read Scripture through our own lens, we miss the insights from the historical church. When we read the Bible outside of community, we can unconsciously twist this passage or that to fit our personal assumptions. One of the biggest lightbulb moments that happens within a mentoring or teaching relationship is that all of the Scriptures are about Jesus. They all point to the completed work of Christ.

After the resurrection, Jesus walked alongside two men on the road to Emmaus (Luke 24:13–35). Their eyes were kept from seeing that the man who accompanied them was Jesus. Before Jesus revealed himself, he first wanted to show them that he was in Scripture and always had been.

> "And he said to them 'O foolish ones, and slow of heart to believe all that the prophets have spoken! Was it not necessary that the Christ should suffer these things and enter into his glory?' And beginning with Moses and all the Prophets, he interpreted to them *in all the Scriptures the things concerning himself.*" (Luke 24:25–27, italics mine).

We can do Bible studies that teach us laws: how to be a better wife, how to be a better person, what this passage says I should do, and what that passage says I should do. But if we do not approach Scripture expecting to understand Christ himself better, we are missing the point.

Scripture can be rightly divided into law and gospel. The law has its work, and the gospel has its work. A good church, and good teachers, will show both the law and gospel. It is evil to feed us law, then more law, then more law, and never show us how Christ is the completion of the law. To give the law without the gospel of Christ is to give us not only exhaustion, but death (2 Cor. 7:10).

We can get stuck on a "conviction high" from churches who teach the law, but do not serve it with the gospel. They say they're just "teaching from Scripture" but they pick and choose which passages will convict us. Through the law, we feel convicted about what is right, we see and understand what is right. We see and want what is right. But to leave it there, or with five steps of application on how to achieve it on your own, is to remove Christ from the Bible reading. When Jesus showed the men on their way to Emmaus, Moses and the prophets, he went all the way back to the beginning of Scripture, as he spoke of Moses, the human hand inspired to write Genesis. The gospel of Jesus does not start in the New Testament. The presence of Jesus does not start in the New Testament. It starts "In the beginning."

"All Scripture is breathed out by God" says 2 Timothy 3:16–17 "and profitable for teaching, for reproof, for correction, and for training in righteousness, that the man of God may be complete, equipped for every good work." The word of God does convict, move, change, and refine us. But none of that is separated from the work of Christ. 2 Timothy, in context, continues on to chapter four, where it says we must be rooted in sound doctrine, endure many things, and tells us how Paul had fought the good fight, and finished the race, and will receive a crown "and not only to me but also to all who have loved his appearing." (2 Tim. 4:8).

When God the Son appeared, to redeem us from our own feeble attempts of self-righteousness, we can rejoice, because as we are in him, we are saved. This is not a return to our self-righteousness; the purpose of Scripture is to root that out of us, and plant us in the sound doctrine of grace through faith. Galatians 2:21, "I do not nullify the grace of God, for if righteousness were through the law, then Christ died for no purpose."

Training in "righteousness" means being trained in Christ's righteousness, because that is the only true righteousness that exists. We don't manufacture it. He bestows it.

We can do Bible reading, but to do it outside of community, outside of good discipleship and preaching, we easily turn Bible study into a conviction marathon, with no gospel. Bible teachers should be trained to identify both law and gospel in the Scriptures, so that they can point to the work of Christ no matter which book a group is studying.

Individual Bible Reading
Feeds into Communal Edification

So, should we abandon individual Bible reading and just go to church? By no means. Reading the Bible is personally edifying, but the blessings and purpose goes further than that. When an individual reads the Bible, it is for the purpose of edifying the whole church. My personal favorite way in Bible reading is to join a weekly Bible study at my church. When I lead a study, the group reads the same chapter of a book we are studying every day of the week. (For instance, we would all read Hebrews chapter 1, each day of the week. The following week, we would read chapter 2 each day.) We write down our notes and questions in a notebook, and then when we meet together, we share our insights, as well as our questions.

This way, we are being daily fed by the actual word of God, but we read not only for our own benefit, but for the benefit of others in the body. This is different than accountability, because if you don't do your reading, you aren't shamed, you simply come and are fed by others when you feel weaker. We are in this together. I can be alone with my thoughts during the daily readings, but I don't keep what God has taught me to myself. A pool of water that does not flow out quickly becomes stagnant and unhealthy. If we want to read more individually, read more freely. It will enrich discussion as we come together as a group and as we disciple others.

Consuming God's Word through Memorization

When we set Bible reading expectations for ourselves, we must remember that the printing press did not exist in biblical times. In fact, it has not existed for the majority of Christianity. Books have historically been expensive, time consuming, and not readily available to the common Christian. This is why it is funny that we say that we must read the Bible by ourselves, when throughout the majority of Christianity, that wasn't even possible for most people. This does not mean that they didn't hear the word. They heard, and they memorized.

Memorization has been a huge comfort for me during the seasons in my life when sitting and reading is a far-off dream. Memorization is not less than or lower in status than reading. We are simply exercising a different part of our brain as we fix our eyes on Jesus. Memorization is something we can do as we are spending hours trying to get babies to sleep. It's something we can do while we are cooking. It's something we can do as we are running errands.

When expectations from others flood my life, memorization is a part of me that others cannot take away. As I'm staring at a lake, I can recite a passage. When I garden, I can ponder the weight of each word. When I drive my kids out to camp, we can sing songs that put Bible verses to music.

There is a horrible mantra that I've heard in education circles in modern times that "you don't have to know; you just need to know where to find it." For instance, these educators would say you don't need to know the dates and names about history, you just know how to find it if you need it. Sadly, the same often gets applied to Scripture. "You don't need to know the verses on love, you just have to know how to search for them." It's a philosophy that is so centered around self and the individual. It approaches Scripture from a pick-and-choose motive, depending on how we would like to use it for our own purposes. It doesn't broaden our horizons or challenge us.

Facts, stories, and memories are passed on in the first stage of learning. We teach toddlers words and language. We tell stories and they parrot our speech. Children who memorize facts do not always know the value of what they memorize. They just enjoy the fun of it. But the next step in education, the logic phase, is when students learn how the facts relate to each other.

How is this fact connected to this fact? Is there a cause and effect? What's the timeline?

Knowing how facts, stories, and experiences relate to each other is how we grow in learning. We simply cannot relate facts that we do not know.

A Picture of the Spirit Using His Word in Individuals for Communal Encouragement

We don't always know when we will use the verses we memorize. Not long ago, I was having one of the long, late night, heart-to-heart conversations with one of my teens, a trademark of this stage of parenting. This particular child has spent years dealing with chronic health conditions, and that evening he was just so fed up with his body and the way that it worked. He was fed up with facing more challenges than my other kids, and he felt like the deck was stacked against him. Self-hatred was sprouting up from the root of these weaknesses he could not seem to shake. The weaknesses ranged from health issues to sin issues, all of which were twisted up together with hormones. He hated that he struggled with sin, with his health, with his mind—all of it.

Some things we can control, and other things we cannot. My son was not about to believe that he was fine just the way he was. In fact, telling him that he was would have made him feel like I was saying that I was fine with him having struggles. Instead, I told my son that when we feel weak, that is when God shows us his strength. I wanted him to know that God loved him, weaknesses and all. I told him we should never hide or cover up our weaknesses from God, but we should bring them to him. Unintentionally, I started to recite several verses on weaknesses, and how God's grace is sufficient for us, even when sometimes the hurt of our weaknesses remains.

I wondered if I was getting through to him. He stared intently at the ground as I spoke. Finally, he quietly recited back to me, "Blessed are the poor in spirit, for theirs is the kingdom of heaven." The Sermon on the Mount that we had memorized years ago together in our little homeschool started coming to the front of his brain, and he spoke the Beatitudes, one after the other. The exact words he needed to hear came pouring out his own mouth.

"Do you feel poor in spirit?" I asked him. He nodded.

"Then God wants you to know that the kingdom of heaven is for you. He doesn't reject you for your broken heart. He goes after it and meets you right where it's broken."

It was a huge breakthrough moment for him. The Holy Spirit brought to mind verse after verse that I spoke to him in our conversation, and then the Holy Spirit brought to his mind more related verses about what we were talking about. The Holy Spirit equipped us through his word and gave us that word in the moment that we needed it. Through that, my son saw the depths of God's love for him, and it softened and encouraged him.

God's dynamic word doesn't just fit into one part of our day. When we memorize his word, it's like we hold the Bible ever in our hands. Memorization offers time in Scripture to those who have no time to sit alone with their Bible. In that way, God gives the greatest to the least. How empowering to realize that when we memorize God's word, no one can separate us from it.

If you struggle to know where to start with memorization, I suggest that you do it with someone, so that you may be mutually encouraged. I was recently working on memorizing Romans 8 with a friend of mine. We both got tripped up on verse 3, fell off the habit for a few weeks, and then one of us said, "let's try that again." We didn't make any promises that we wouldn't face more interruptions, or that we wouldn't forget again. We just decided to take the next verse together.

I also suggest that you memorize whole chunks of Scripture, instead of random verses. I have many random verses in me, and they bless me as well. But to memorize a whole book, even if it's small, or to memorize a whole chapter, puts the word of God *in context* into your mind. There will be fewer temptations to twist God's word to your own purposes when you know the truth of what comes before and after that verse.

Second, I recommend that you don't memorize in order to get "the basic idea" but, rather, memorize each word carefully, as a scribe would write out the Bible in a monastery. Is it "a" or "the?" Was that "fruit" or "fruits?" Once a section is memorized, read through that section again, every so often, to make sure you remember the specifics. Like noticing the details in a painting—the nuances in Scripture details are beautiful and can change whole perspectives.

Third, I recommend that you would treat this discipline as you would prayer or fasting. Don't broadcast it, brag about it, or let it interfere with serving your neighbors. I have struggled with pride when it comes to memorization more than I have with any other discipline. Because of this, I don't often track my memorization progress, or keep track of how many chapters or verses I have memorized. My Bible-memorization partners know my weakness in this and are sensitive to it. I want the focus to be in the awe of how many words God gave us, not how many words I can remember. For me, it's like being an alcoholic who can't have just one drink. Some people can keep track of their progress and be encouraged. I keep track of my progress and get puffed up. If I memorize a chapter over the course of a year, or over the course of a month, I surely have no idea, but I keep going after that next verse.

Cut off the pride, and let it just be what it is: the Holy Spirit working in you, to equip you for good works. Obviously, if you are doing this with someone else, this will not be a "secret." There is a place between "secret" and "broadcasting," and it is good to be there.

How do you memorize sections of Scripture? I have found the easiest way is to read the sections over and over again, until they settle into me. Once I've read that passage many times, I try to say the first line. Maybe the next day, I read the whole passage again, and then recite it from the beginning, seeing if I can get a line further. Some people give themselves deadlines, but I don't. Just one line further, sometimes more. Whatever God enables me to do that day.

Many months will go by when I don't memorize anything new, and I will simply *use* what I've memorized in my daily life and in my vocation. Then I will find myself aching for some more memorization. I'll read my Bible for a while, sometimes more months, until I find a passage that I know I need in me for that season. I'll get stuck there for sometimes a week or two, or sometimes a year or two, until it's memorized. God is not rushed.

Artificial timelines are sometimes helpful, and other times they are just one more stress in our lives. If you struggle with knowing how much or how often you should memorize, ask for the Holy Spirit to guide you. Ask him to interrupt you when you're overdoing it and neglecting a different part of your vocation. Ask him to remind you when you forget to memorize. These are things that we can ask the Spirit of God and he graciously and eagerly does them. In fact, depend on him as much as you can. I get giddy sometimes just seeing how much he cares about me in this, when I feel like I should be doing this for him. But no, he does this *for me*. He is *for us* and given to us to *help us*. There are no bonus points for relying on him less. He is not impressed by us showing off what we can do on our own. In fact, I am pretty sure he would think that is actually counterproductive to the goal of greater dependence on Christ.

CHAPTER 9

Prayer

"My dear God, how stupid we people are until You give us something. Even in praying it is You who have to pray in us. I would like to write a beautiful prayer but I have nothing to do it from. There is a whole sensible world around me that I should be able to turn to Your praise; but I cannot do it. Yet at some insipid moment when I may possibly be thinking of floor wax or pigeon eggs, the opening of a beautiful prayer may come up from my subconscious and lead me to write something exalted. I am not a philosopher or I could understand these things."

—FLANNERY O'CONNER
A PRAYER JOURNAL[1]

THE HOLY SPIRIT INTERPRETS my groans. With all of our books on prayer, with all of our academic analysis of passages like the Lord's Prayer, with all of our organizational systems for keeping track of intercessory prayer lists, instructions for praying Scripture, prayer chains—a multitude of resources out there—I find the most comfort in knowing that when all is said and done, the Holy Spirit interprets my groans.

I have gone through seasons of preferring different praying methods. I went through the formula-prayer season. Adoration, Confession, Thanksgiving, Supplication. (ACTS). There are many other formulas available as well. I like to call it "make sure all your bases are covered" prayer.

Some pattern their prayer after the Lord's Prayer. Make sure you're doing and saying the things you should be doing and saying. It is not wrong to be catechized in the elements of prayer. For someone who has no idea where to start, this is an excellent teaching tool. It shows all the things you *can* do in prayer, and helps us exercise those things, and remember that it's not just about us and asking for stuff, but giving God the glory.

I have kept detailed prayer lists, where each prayer item has a box next to it to check once that prayer has been answered. I have also collected prayer requests on 3x5 index cards and filed them in a little box where I would pray through them. I have wept with emotion in prayer.

I have prayed aloud in groups, awkwardly trying to find the right words so I don't sound stupid. I have blanked, many times in these groups, and have just ended it with "in Jesus name" to end my discomfort. I have learned the secret code—which prayerful things are acceptable in each group, the prayer lingo for letting the next person know it's their turn. I have done "popcorn prayer" where we just say random things to God in a circle, until the leader closes it up.

I have prayed and wondered if I was just talking to myself. I have prayed and felt nothing. I have prayed dutifully before I eat my food, and then been unable to remember if I just prayed or not.

I have prayed over people who need it, and I've been prayed over, as people laid hands on me and begged for healing. I have prayed over someone oppressed by a demon in Jesus' name, and saw an extreme, instant change in them when I commanded the demon to leave.

I have kept prayer journals where I write out my thoughts, so that I can maintain focus and not fall asleep in the early morning hours. I have prayed the Scriptures and have written down Bible verses translated to prayer in journals for each of my children that I read and pray when I'm discouraged.

I have argued with God out loud in an empty field on our farm. I have been angry with him and yelled at him. I have disagreed with him and how he's handling a situation with someone I love. I have read aloud pre-written prayers in old books and found comfort that some old saint has already written the words that I want to say but can't think of in my moment of need.

There are many methods of prayer, but what astonishes me more than any of them, is that the Holy Spirit interprets my groans. I can groan, and God not only hears me, but understands me. When we talk about the level of intimacy God is offering us through prayer, I think that's a good place to start. Please don't ask me the correct way to groan.

The Mercy Seat

When my husband and I were first married, we taught 2nd grade Sunday school at our church together. We were given a curriculum to teach, and each week the book laid out four activities to do. Our class time usually allowed only one or two of those activities to happen. I usually wanted to pick whatever activities on the list were calm and quiet. That didn't usually go well for a little blonde-headed kid in class named John.

John was full of questions, and he rarely drew breath between them. He was not mean or disobedient, but he was precocious and busy. He definitely kept us on our toes, and we often had him in mind when we planned our class, because if John wasn't kept busy, no one would learn anything. One evening as Knut (my husband) and I planned our lesson, we read about an activity that would require us to make a 3D model of the temple. All the little paper pieces were provided, but the project still looked like it would take a long time and a high level of involvement.

"Let's do this one!" Knut's eyes lit up.

"That would take forever to set up. Let's do this coloring page instead." I lazily replied.

"No, no. We have to do this one. It's too good of an opportunity to pass up," He settled it.

"Suit yourself," I said.

My sweet husband, with his large hands, spent hours cutting and gluing the bitty pieces of paper together with all the assembly instructions for hours that night.

The next morning during Sunday school, we went through the lesson, and when we got to the point where we brought out the 3D model, the curriculum prompted us to ask the children a few questions. They couldn't have even taken five minutes to answer. I read and reread the page. That can't be it. Knut didn't spend hours the night before to just have a few passing comments and then move on.

I was determined to make the most of his tedious offering.

So, I gathered the kids close, and I told them I was going to show them all the parts of the whole 3D model. Knut and I had each gone to Bible school, so we went off script and pieced together what we knew. We started telling the kids about the parts of the temple that we thought we could explain correctly.

"This part is where the sacrifices would take place."

"Right here is the Holy place. Only priests could go in there."

"And here is the Holy of Holies. Only the high priest could go in there, and only on the Day of Atonement. My pastor growing up told me that they would tie a rope around him when he went in, in case he died in the presence of the Lord, and the other priests could pull him out."

The boys' eyes grew wide.

We explained that the Holy of Holies contained the Ark of the Covenant, a box covered in gold. Inside the box was the 10 commandments, manna that the Lord had provided, and Aaron's staff that had sprouted. His law, his nourishment, his new life out of a dead thing. On top of this golden box were 2 golden seraphim, heavenly beings, kind of like angels, positioned in such a way to point to the glory— (the presence—) of God. These wings on the seraphim served as a throne-like image called the "Mercy Seat." The mercy seat is where the presence of God would rest, and the high priest could meet with God there on the Day of Atonement.

We explained to our captive audience that the book of Hebrews shows that this temple was just an imprint, a shadow of God's dwelling place in heaven. The mercy seat in that Holy of Holies was simply something visual for us to see, we told the boys, because we could not see the real mercy seat where God is ruling forever. Yet the Old Testament temple held that it had such holiness that priests could die going in there, if they went in without being covered by the sacrifice.

I pointed to the doorway into the Holy of Holies. A thick curtain separated this small room, (the Holy of Holies) from the outer room (the Holy place), where the rest of the priests could assemble.

I don't know why I said it. It didn't have anything to do with the lesson or the curriculum. But I said, "When Jesus' gave his last breath on the cross, there was an earthquake, and the curtain that restricted access to the Holy of Holies was torn from top to bottom."

John had been silent this whole time. He was taking it all in. But here he interrupted. He said quietly and full of wonder mixed with fear, "Then anyone could get to God!"

The pause hung in the room as all the kids let that idea sink in.

"That's right. Then anyone could get to God. You see how big a deal that was, right?"

It took a lot to make John silent.

The final sacrifice had been made. The privilege of being able to speak with God who sits upon the mercy seat, is available to all of us.

Take a moment to ponder the name God gave his throne: "Mercy Seat," where God sits in his mercy to meet with us. When you pray, you are praying to the God who walked with Adam and Eve, the God of Abraham, Isaac, and Jacob. You're talking to the God of Ruth, the God who gave Jonah over to a large fish, and the God who parted the seas for Moses, Elijah, and Elisha. When you pray, you are praying to the God who was born as a human baby, and yet remained fully God, who knows what it is to be human, knows what it's like to live within skin, be tempted, and feel the most torturous pain. Jesus had emotions. He knows. When you pray, you pray to the God who sits upon the mercy seat.

And he wants to talk with you.

What Is Prayer?

Martin Luther writes to his friend, "I'll do my best to show you how I approach prayer. May our Lord God help us all do better in this regard.

Amen. First, sometimes I feel I am being cold and apathetic about prayer. This is usually because of all the things that are distracting me and filling my mind. I know this is a result of the flesh and the devil always waging war against me, trying to prevent me from praying."[2]

We all know it's a good thing to pray. Luther points out two reasons that we don't do it: our flesh and the devil.

I don't know how I can address prayer without addressing the spiritual warfare attached to it. This is where I battle in my own life. This is where I have experienced demonic attacks. This is where I struggle with doubt and disappointment. I'm not always in the mood to pray, and yet praying is my greatest comfort. I am an emotional, sensitive person. Somehow, I think that makes me unreliable to write about prayer. I want to give you something stronger than my own flawed experience. But prayer must be connected to experience. In prayer, we recognize the Eternal One in a finite, present moment.

God has been so gentle with me in prayer. Does that mean he is like that with everyone? I don't know. There is only a handful of times that I have been "brought low" in prayer, experiencing an intense humbling. Each time, I had arrogance that needed addressing.

If prayer is a conversation, it's important to remember that God is speaking, so keep your Bible nearby. Prayer affects our knowledge and understanding of Scripture, and we look through the lens of Scripture to gain our knowledge of prayer. Scripture and prayer are inseparable.

God knows the challenges we face and our own limitations in assessing his message for us.

- Did God say . . . ?
- Is God trying to tell me . . . ?

We struggle to trust our emotions. But prayer isn't some type of sadistic test of our ability to practice "hearing God . . . maybe." Open your Bible, and have confidence that God isn't trying to trick you or leave you open to deception. He's right there. He has spoken and his word is living and active (Heb. 4:12). He knows what you need to hear.

I bare all of my sin, both the intentional and unintentional, in prayer. The Holy Spirit loosens and convicts the sin I cling to as I pray, and my prayer becomes a confession.

Is that how it's supposed to work with everyone? I come to prayer more often with an agenda of what I wish to accomplish, which sometimes gets accomplished, but it's often more enjoyable if I pray just to talk, with no agenda at all—just for the sheer enjoyment of talking with God. Does that mean you have to do it that way? Not necessarily.

Many approach the subject of prayer from a logic and reason perspective. They ask "does it work?," and I would respond with the question, "What's your definition of 'work?' What are you expecting prayer to accomplish?"

If we define "prayer works" to mean that God gives us whatever we want like spoiled children, we will be disappointed. God is not Santa Claus. If we mean "prayer works" to mean that our intimacy with God will increase, I think we are closer. But how on earth does one describe talking with God? I asked this question to my aunt, who has for many years been a mentor of mine. She texted back, "forget logistics. You learn as you go. That's how it works."

As we embrace mystery in the sacraments, as we wrestle with the physical and metaphysical, and try to clearly define what is happening and how it is happening, we may end up frustrated. Should we expect any interaction with God to be anything less than supernatural or full of mystery we don't quite understand? We aren't given full explanations as to how prayer works, how it changes things, or what exactly our role is. We just know that because of the sacrifice of Jesus, our high priest, God invites us into the Holy of Holies, to his mercy seat.

That's the thing about prayer. We approach God imperfectly. We approach him as sinners wearing the covering of Christ. There cannot be any pretense about it. Pretense is in opposition to intimacy. We are who we are, and God is who he is. Don't flower it up or try to be impressive. God will teach you as you go. Use written prayers if it helps. Write out prayers if it helps. Use the prayers of poets if they resonate.

It is most wonderful to use the Bible in prayer, even praying some verses that you need help understanding, or praying verses in the hopes that they would sink into your soul and cause you to believe them. The sacraments of baptism and the Lord's Supper, they are empty gestures apart from the word. But when the word and the physical acts are brought together, something sacred happens, and we don't often understand the "how" of it all.

This topic of prayer mystifies academics. It does not fit into a tidy syllogism. Is it logical and formulaic, or is it emotional and instinctive? Both—that's the crazy part. To pray is to spend time with One whose logic is above our own and to remind us that faith is not dependent on what we see.

Our limited understanding of prayer does not need to inhibit us. In fact, I think sometimes the only way to understand is to just pray. Groan, if you must. Your understanding will grow, but your confidence in "knowing" will not. The more we learn about God, the more we are humbled by his majesty beyond what we comprehend.

The Holy Spirit Rooting Our Minds in Christ

Consider the Holy Spirit as a wind (John 3:8). We can't see the wind, but we can feel the effects of the wind. With this in mind, I invite you to view the rustling leaves of the Psalms. The psalmists' emotions sway as they try to make sense of the world. God inspires words that shows the movement of the Holy Spirit upon the human psyche. Each psalm rests the emotions of the psalmists in the sanity and surety of who God is. People bring chaos. The Spirit brings Christ. You can see the Spirit work upon the heart of the psalmist on each page.

In the Psalms we see a variety of emotions, such as fear, uncertainty, anger, and joy. We can see the action of the Spirit form the thinking of the psalmists from chaos into the ordered peace of knowing that God is sovereign, and he holds them. You never hear David say "I probably shouldn't have said that" though what he says sometimes makes us, the readers, cringe. David exposed every part of his heart, and it wasn't always pretty.

God's promise to be with us isn't purely theoretical or academic. It is real and tangible. We pour out our hearts, and as he hears us, he helps us. Sometimes he changes our circumstances. Other times he changes and teaches our hearts. The emotions of prayer depend on our moods or circumstances, but the effect of prayer is much more profound than simply emotional experiences. Emotions may be a byproduct, but what we experience through prayer isn't relegated to the simple categories of so much happy or sad. The emotions associated with prayer may be described as hatred letting go of the vice on our hearts, humility seeping into our understanding, praise rushing to our lips in wonder, compassion growing for our enemies, justice rising up within us for victims with no advocate, or a peaceful resignation into trusting who God is.

The Details

Does God encourage long or short prayers? What time of day is most optimal? What method is best? Before we can address the "how" of our lives, we must first understand the "why." When we understand the "why" and understand that God uses whatever we offer him, we will look to see what he does through it. This is very different than looking to see how we can manipulate prayer to our best advantage. Once again, we must fix our eyes on Jesus, the author and perfecter of our faith, not our works and methods.

Jesus is very clear that God is not impressed by our performances in prayer. The Lord's Prayer is profoundly short and simple. On the other hand, God calls us to be persistent (Luke 18:1–8). These ideas are not in opposition, rather God showing us that we do not need to make our prayers long for his sake. But we should never feel like we are bothering him in our persistence. God is a storyteller, and we are his children whose souls long for a continuous diet of stories. Through prayer, God sows a story of his work in our own life, and we are mere participants.

When Paul says, "pray continually," or sometimes translated "pray without ceasing," he's employing hyperbole to shows the reality of our unending union with Christ. Pray all the time. "Screw pragmatics" as my aunt so eloquently said. Just start. Don't wait to feel a certain emotion, for the best circumstances, for the right words, or anything else of it. The Holy Spirit will correct you along the way, don't worry. If you don't know what to say, just open your Bible and start asking honest questions. Don't be afraid to wrestle with the text. The power that he teaches in prayer isn't something we manage, but something he does in us as we learn the depths of his love.

God Wants to Bring Our Attention to His Works.

"The important thing, the real goal of study, is the 'development of attention.' Why? Because *prayer consists of attention*, and all worldly study is really a stretching of the soul towards prayer."[3]

In his book on classical education Stratford Caldecott writes about the importance of training a student's mind to hold attention, because attention is the posture of prayer. If this is true, perhaps our struggle to focus on anything that does not give instant gratification is a direct assault on our prayer life.

God is never in a rush. He does not meet with us for our amusement, though I find he has a sense of humor. He does not prioritize getting us through prayer quickly, or even getting through it uninterrupted. Prayer is not a box to check in order to please God. Prayer is paying attention to the works of God.

As we sit, stand, or go throughout our days in our own vocations, we can become consumed with what we accomplish. To pray continually is to keep our minds present to the fact that God has not left us. God will never leave us. God is here to help us. He is not there as a tool in our tool belts, to be maneuvered and used to accomplish our goals. The mere awareness of the presence of God throughout our day reminds us of the multitude of his works—and not just what he is capable of doing, but why he does them. He does them as an outpouring of love—his very nature.

Say a prayer, ask for help, share your heart, confess your sin, be present to the wonder that the curtain was torn. Anyone has access to God by the sacrifice of Jesus.

Prayer in Community

With our righteousness secure in Christ, the only thing left for us to do is love God and love our neighbor, which includes praying for your neighbor. Jesus tells us to even pray for those who persecute you (Matt. 5:44). We often hear calls for prayers for healing when people are sick. Some of the most awful physical trials are when people wrestle with the sovereignty and goodness of God. It is good to wrestle with God's decisions for healing of people, and through prayer. Prayer is where we can meet him together.

The Bible also talks about praying for one another after confession, and through the process of confession, because it brings healing. Many relationships have been healed through prayer. I find that praying for someone else trains me not to manipulate others. It is good to talk with people who have offended you. But there are many circumstances when the confrontation will blow up in your face, and it is very wise to pray.

I can think of various situations on social media when I will write and post something as non-controversial as possible, and someone just has to come in and comment something wildly controversial, just to get a rise out of people. In one scenario, I thought of my options. I could delete the inflammatory comment, which would lead to the commenter screaming "censorship!" louder. Or, I could leave it up, and leave the door open for my diverse group of friends to attack the poor person who wanted to say something harsh and would now get publicly whipped for it. Lastly, I could pray for them, that the Holy Spirit would convict them for their words. Nearly every time I have taken the final approach, the next time I check my post, they've deleted their comment on their own.

I've learned that, as a mother, I have the tendency to lecture from my vastly superior wisdom, especially as my kids are getting older. I do it too much, and my kids' eyes glaze over. Sometimes my children obey me with their actions, but I can tell their hearts are far from obedience. That's when I have to remind myself—I don't have access to people's hearts. I don't have the ability to see people's hearts and change people's hearts. Me? I only have manipulative tactics to get what I want. That doesn't usually turn out well. When my children's hearts are far from me, I've learned to close my mouth to lectures, stop throwing my own tantrums, and just pray. "Holy Spirit, you have access to their hearts. Soften their hearts towards me (or their siblings). Help me to be tender and honorable with any influence towards them I have."

It's not just that prayer works, it's that God's ways are just so much better and effective than our ways. The Holy Spirit is so much more potent and efficient than my tactics to reach people's hearts. Prayer works because God is good, and God is able. Prayer's effectiveness has nothing to do with my beautiful formation of words, or my will being the dominant will.

If God has called me to pray for someone, it doesn't matter who they are or what they did, I know that he will pull the hatred out of my heart in the process. I will be completely unable to remain hardened towards them. My prayer life is not always pretty, and I don't feel like I'm a shining example. I'm too snarky with God; I'm too lazy, and I confess a lot of sin during prayer. The Holy Spirit points me to the truth of my sin a lot during prayer, and points me to Christ consistently, and it's hard. But I have seen God do amazing things through prayer, both for me, and for other people, because he is just that good, and he is just that loving.

We have access to come before the mercy seat. We can come together, and we can come individually. God cares about our relationships, and he will see to it that love is poured out on us. He is the one who has the access and ability to change hearts, so don't wait to feel deserving and don't wait for others to be deserving, before you bring any of it before the throne of God. We can cast all our cares on him, because he truly does care for us.

CHAPTER 10

Meditation

"Meditation is the activity of calling to mind, and thinking over, and dwelling on, and applying to oneself, the various things that one knows about the works and ways and purposes and promises of God. It is an activity of holy thought, consciously performed in the presence of God, under the eye of God, by the help of God, as a means of communion with God."

—J.I. PACKER
"KNOWING GOD"[1]

WOULDN'T IT BE SO much easier to respond, "Well, just read your Bible and pray every day," when asked the question, "how do I be a spiritual Christian?" That little checklist is looking pretty good right now. Just read a chapter, recite a prayer, and move on with your day. Once we understand that spirituality isn't something we do or accomplish, but something we *receive*, then we must brace ourselves for the fact that when God gives, he gives in abundance. He will not save halfway. It will look deeper, more invasive, and more transformative than we could have dreamed.

The baptismal water will find every crack and crevice of our hearts, and no part of our lives will be untouched. This is not about grabbing wisdom nuggets in five-minute chunks here and there so that you can live an effective and productive life. Simply put, meditation is when we think.

In a world of predigested data, spoon fed in mini doses, the practice of thinking can be scary.

- What if I think the wrong thing?
- What if I come across something I don't understand?
- What if my doubts can't be addressed, and overtake my faith?

We don't want to feel dumb. We don't want to face our hardest questions. We worry God will ask too much of us. We don't want to rock the boat. So, we push to accomplish a task, say the prayer, read the chapter. That way, we know that we did our jobs, no one could say otherwise. We also keep busy—very busy. So busy that we can't or won't stop and think about God.

We resist meditation because we instinctively know what comes after it, and we don't know if we have the time or strength to do it.

Luther's Meditation

Christian meditation looks nothing like the meditation of Yogis or New Agers. There is nothing in Christian meditation about emptying yourself or your mind. As the rest of the disciplines directed by the Holy Spirit, meditation has everything to do with pointing to Christ. In Christian meditation, we dwell on the story of Christ.

Christian meditation is centered on the word of God, and the way Luther put it, meditation is like rubbing an herb to release the flavor.[2] I love that image. I have a mint plant outside my front door. To rub it is to feel its ridges, to be calmed by its softness, and to be awakened by its potent smell. I can taste the leaf, chew on its sharp flavor, and eat it.

Inward Meditation

In Luther's monastic life, he was taught 3 phases of reaching some kind of enlightenment or understanding. Those 3 steps were: prayer, meditation, and enlightenment. First, the monks would pray that the Holy Spirit would reveal to them what the Scriptures meant. Then they would meditate on the Scriptures, pondering them wholly. Then they would wait for enlightenment to arrive.

After the Reformation, Luther edited this process for his reformed brethren: prayer, meditation, temptation. Though he uses that Latin word for temptation (which can be confusing as our modern English ear thinks Luther means God tempting us to sin, which he doesn't do) he clarifies what he means with the German word for "battle or attack." (*anfechtung*)[3]

As a scholar, it would be easy for Luther to approach the Scriptures simply as an academic, but he insists that we can twist them to our own logic and reason unless—through prayer—we are asking for the Holy Spirit to open our eyes to see and understand them. Prayer is a necessary part of Bible reading. We are not left to just figure it out on our own.

Then comes meditation. We often resist meditation by keeping ourselves busy because we know what comes next. The third step: *anfechtung*. He writes "For as soon as God's Word takes root and grows in you, the devil will harry you, and will make a real doctor [of theology] of you, and by his assaults will teach you to seek and love God's Word."[4]

So much for having daily devotions making your life "easier." According to Luther, you pray for understanding, you meditate on the word, and then you can expect a time of refining, of wrestling, of arguing, and coming to terms with what is true. I find this process incredibly grace filled. We are allowed to struggle. We shouldn't be ashamed of asking God questions, or maybe even doubting. Some of us do not go calmly into belief. Luther found that most of us wrestle. He found that God often allows uncomfortable circumstances for us to exercise the truth of what we are reading. And it's not only okay to wrestle, we should expect to wrestle as a result of meditating on God's word. God knows what we need to understand deep in our bones. We understand what God says is true most often through fire, where we see all other systems and idols burn away. What God reveals to be true remains.

> "This is the touchstone which teaches you not only to know and understand, but also to experience how right, how true, how sweet, how lovely, how mighty, how comforting God's Word is, wisdom beyond all wisdom."[5]

In other words, we use prayer as we read God's Word to help us understand the text, then we meditate on God's Word. As the meaning of God's words takes root in our hearts through the power of the Holy Spirit, God provides opportunities for their truth to be tested in real life, in real time. God is not hurting you. On the contrary, God allows Satan to "harry us" so that we can experience the power of the words he just gave us.

Another way of saying these 3 stages:

1) These are the words *for you.*
2) This is what they *mean.*
3) This is what they're *for.*

> "Count it all joy, my brothers, when you meet trials of various kinds, for you know that the testing of your faith produces

steadfastness. And let steadfastness have its full effect, that you may be perfect and complete, lacking in nothing." (James 1:2–4)

When we pray for understanding, God's answers are multifaceted. He will give us our faith. He will tell us what faith is. Then he will show us its strength, not so he can see its strength, but so we can see.

How frustrated Satan must be to be used in this way. Every attack of hatred he lashes at us grows us to a deeper understanding of the power of God's love. Every low blow, every temptation, every hurt roots us in beautiful dependence in God Almighty. Everything he does, God redeems for our sake, thus putting Satan in a lose-lose situation. God doesn't show us this power so that we can build ourselves a little kingdom here on earth, with all of the riches and comforts we could want. God shows us this firm power of faith because the Devil is real, and grace through faith has defeated any hold he has on us.

Does this mean we should shrug our shoulders when the Devil attacks one of our brothers and sisters, and say, "Well, God will redeem that. Let's just let them work through that." Does knowing this make us apathetic? By no means! There is no place in the Bible where God promises us that we will never be tempted, that there will be no hardship, no difficulty, or any of that. In fact, we should expect it. We should only be comforted to know it's a process that promises to refine us, and God is not caught off guard or surprised by it.

Outward Meditation

Because of the depth of Luther's wrestling in isolation, he was even more adamant that we don't just focus on inward meditation, but outward meditation. It was Luther who lived in this time of renaissance and had spent many years of his life in monastic inward meditation, did all the things monks did, and when he found grace, he changed. From then on, he taught, practiced, and encouraged people to embrace and find comfort in outward meditation.

Outward meditation can be found within a community, as we meditate upon God's word as receivers. "Luther envisages the practice of meditation primarily as an outward physical activity. As such, meditation is inspired by the Divine Service [a church service]. There, God's Word is enacted publicly in Confession and Absolution, in proclamation and Benediction, in prayer and praise, in adoration and in celebration of Holy Communion. God commands the Church to preach, read, hear, sing, and speak His Word, so that through it He can deliver His Holy Spirit to His people. Therefore, the enactment of God's Word in the Divine Service determines how and on what we meditate."[6]

To put it plainly, Luther says we meditate when we go to church, and participate in receiving God's gifts. We sing the songs that the musicians play. We hear a sermon. We receive the benediction. We receive communion, and not in rote movements to please God, but to understand that we are not doing this Christian life alone by our own power. And yet, God doesn't just interact with us corporately, but individually we receive grace there.

We don't have to wrestle alone. We don't have to wrestle in isolation. It's important to remember that, as God gives us himself *for us*, that doesn't mean for me, and me alone. We are one body.

Logical and Imaginative

As we think upon the word of God and seek to understand its meaning, it is not only important, but a delight to think fully. Depending on if you are a right-brain or a left-brain dominant thinker, you may find more delight in thinking critically and logically about God, or you may approach Scriptures more imaginatively. From an educational perspective, we can easily settle into whatever approach most naturally suits our brains and learning styles. Might I suggest that looking through both lenses—logic and imagination—helps us see most clearly.

Like most people, Jesus loved a good story. Like a great teacher, he used stories a lot. Stories bring nuance and paint a full-color picture in a world that just says, "give me the black and white rules and leave me alone." When God gave the law, he wrote it in stone. When God gave the gospel, he told a story. It's not a to-do list, or a don't-do list. It's the story of redemption. It's the story of God coming down to us. Whenever people tried to get a set of rules out of Jesus, or tried to debate which rules were the most important, or which ones should we focus on, he would repeat the rules in a way that almost sounded hyperbolic to our ears, in the extreme high standard of God. Then he told a story of grace and restoration, of finding what was lost, of giving what wasn't earned.

C.S. Lewis talks at great lengths in several books about the logical thinking within Christianity and tries to rationally work through the idea of how prayer "works." But he also talks about the baptism of his imagination.[7] Before you call me heretical, let me explain that when he was an atheist, Lewis read the works of George MacDonald. The stories were so well written, so imaginative, that for the first time, Lewis could come to terms with the idea that the story of the Bible could be true. While some use apologetics and logic to defend the faith, there are those that use a baptized imagination to do the same thing, for the other side of the brain that is very closely attached to our hearts. God doesn't just want our rational side or our imaginative side. He wants all of us.

The message of the gospel can be understood through the logical syllogisms within Lewis' book *Mere Christianity*, but it is also on display through the imaginative portal into Narnia. In fact, it may be unwise to restrict ourselves to just one part of our brain when wanting to understand the depths of God's love. Through our baptism, God claims all of it.

I was a child who "wasted" so much time daydreaming. Daydreaming was my favorite pastime. I have learned with my own children that three years old is when their imagination peaks to hilarious proportions. They have trouble distinguishing between what is real and what is imaginative at that age. It is the age when they pretend to be a puppy for two weeks, but also the age that they get night terrors. What is real? One of my children I actually worried about for a while, because what she imagined was so vivid that she couldn't distinguish between real and imaginary until she was about seven. And yet, children are a delight to our Father with their imaginations. Their willingness to believe the impossible through the power of story pleases him.

Children are masters of using imagination and wonder to make sense of their world. My six-year-old once came inside after playing in our yard and said she was thinking about God and wondered why he gave her legs that ran so fast. She decided that God was very thoughtful to give her legs, because without them, she would have to bounce everywhere, and bouncing is much more tiring and would smush our tummies, and God knew that bouncing from place to place would not be good for us. As I said, children are masters of meditation. They love to think about things, and not just what is, but what is possible.

Logic comes with skepticism, and imagination comes with the ability to wonder, and both are good and needed when meditating on God's word. We have to say, "wait, that didn't sound right. What's the context? What is it really saying?" We also have to say, "I wonder if that extends to this." When we wonder about biblical truths or texts, our brain can put those abstract thoughts into concrete images which any educator can tell you moves those thoughts from the short-term memory to the long-term memory in our brains.

> "With the eyes of our heart, with *imagination*, we grasp the reality of the kingdom of God, even though we cannot yet see it fully. But we live in an age in which things like faith, spirit, and imagination are widely rejected because they are impossible to prove with the senses. We are taught to distrust anything we cannot observe, quantify, and prove, and this viewpoint seeps into the way we teach children to encounter the world around them and the longing in their heart."[8]

A Picture of Everyday Meditation

I recently attended my nephew's baptism at a Catholic church. As a Protestant, I don't find myself in Catholic spaces often, but I have some experience. My old college campus was a Catholic monastery before it became a Protestant college, and it had a stunning chapel on the grounds, with intricately designed stations of the cross around the perimeter of the interior. I loved studying in that chapel, with its perfect acoustics, walking around and admiring the beauty. It was a lovely place to pray. When I traveled to France a couple of years back to visit a friend, I toured an old church in the little town of Albertville and walked the stations of the cross, marked by paintings hanging on the wall.

I wasn't able to visit as many cathedrals in Europe as I wanted during that trip, but I was able to get a quick visit to John Calvin's home church in Geneva, Switzerland, before I flew home. It was a Catholic cathedral before John Calvin's time. The church is known for its plainness, but entering the sanctuary immediately lifted my eyes and caused me to gasp in wonder.

Walking the stations of the cross is an example of the historic "spiritual discipline of meditation." I often wonder if Luther enjoyed this as a pastime, as he contemplated the work of the cross.

The discipline of meditation is a restful training, as the brain sits in wonder over something God has done. Sometimes this turns into wrestling, as we often disagree with God, but that is part of the training too. In all the biblical commands to meditate on God's word, the meaning of that word is "muse, imagine, ponder, moan, complain." God allows us to wrestle with truths about him.

That's why I love walking the stations of the cross. Remember, before the Bible was available to buy at the store, in the days when much of the congregation was illiterate, and the printing press had not yet been invented, the word of God was read aloud. Christians heard God's word, but besides a small, elite class of scholars, most did not read it. To help the congregation remember these stories and dwell on them, artists would make stained glass windows that told stories, or mosaics, marble carvings, or paintings like these stations of the cross so that people could quietly meditate—I wonder about what it must have been like.

Here's how it went for me this last time, as I followed my squirmy toddler around the stations of the cross during his cousin's baptism. I came to the picture of Simon of Cyrene helping Jesus carry the cross. I started to wonder why God included this story in the Bible. I pondered the significance (Mark 15:21). Why would it be important to include that someone had to *help* Jesus carry the cross? Wow. Isn't that a statement? Jesus needed help saving the world? That doesn't sound right.

At the same time that I wondered this, I heard the priest behind me continue on the baptism, stating the Catholic reasons for Jesus' own baptism. Then my mind wandered back to wondering at Simon carrying Jesus' cross. Jesus wasn't baptized because he was a sinner. He was baptized because it was part of God's plan. Likewise, Jesus wasn't helped on his way to crucifixion because our God is needy, but because him being helped was part of God's plan. Why would God include this?

My wonder then drifted to all the times that I have to accept help from people, when I would rather just be sufficient alone. I would rather stand on my own two feet, and yet, I need help. I hate accepting help. I'm trying to get better at accepting it when people offer. Yet, it's . . . humbling.

Jesus needed help, and yet he did not sin. That made me pause. *Needing help isn't sinful, because Jesus was without sin.* Therefore, it isn't wrong to accept help. The wonder continued.

So, did Jesus accept help to show me that I should accept help? No, it's more than that. Accepting help is humbling. Jesus was being humbled further on the way to the cross. I paused and wept a little inside.

Jesus, is there any humiliation you skipped that day? Even a little?

My mind then jumped straight to Philippians 2, memorized long ago, which talks about the voluntary humbling that Jesus took upon himself.

Jesus made himself needy enough to need help as a part of the humbling process, which was ultimately part of the salvation story.

So how does God use me accepting help as a means of disciplining me to be humble? Does he allow me to be needy for my spiritual good, so that I'm in a position where help is needed, and I'm aware in concrete ways of my need for God?

Then my toddler ran some more, and I moved on to the next station of the cross.

Meditation is letting your brain be in wonder about the acts of God. When God is drawing you to meditation, you'll know the signs that it is God at work because you will find yourself pointed to the Scriptures and the person of Christ.

Just like meditating on the Simon of Cyrene painting led me to worship yet another sacrifice of self-dignity that Jesus did for me, it also led me to remember a Scripture passage (Phil. 2) which I was able to read again that night, to verify my earlier thoughts.

I then began reflecting on the gifts that are brought to a congregation when God brings in artists, musicians, and poets, and I wondered at their purpose in the church. The stations of the cross are made by artists for the purpose of igniting our imaginations to meditate and to wonder. The cathedral I visited in Geneva, designed by architects, ignited my imagination to wonder upon the beauty and goodness of the Lord. Music with words that give beautiful images convey truth in ways our mind can understand.

Poetry paints images across our imagination to help us understand the vast nature of God's love; sermons, illustrations and logical explanations help us understand the depth of a passage. Stories like those of C.S. Lewis' Narnia and others move these abstract stories and ideas of God to concrete images that relate specifically to each generation, each culture, every tribe, and person. Meditation is the natural outcome of the Holy Spirit working through the vocation of preachers, apologists, poets, and artists within the church. God will use prompts everywhere to cause us to *think*, to cause us to wonder, and drive us back to Scripture to understand them deeper. To God be the glory.

CHAPTER 11

Fasting

"Fasting, like the gospel, isn't for the self-sufficient and those who feel they have it all together. It's for the poor in spirit. It's for those who mourn. For the meek. For those who hunger and thirst for righteousness. In other words, fasting is for Christians. It's a desperate measure, for desperate times, among those who know themselves desperate for God."

—DAVID MATHIS
HABITS OF GRACE[1]

AS I'VE WRITTEN THIS book, I have come to complete standstills more than once. I research. I pray. I make notes and more notes. I try to focus on something else and read some fiction. I'll work on this chapter, and then that one. Sometimes I'm stuck. It's not writer's block. I have words. They're rambling and chaotic and full of self. I'm stuck. Sometimes I write out a paragraph and realize that none of the words are worth sharing. They are empty and bring no value to the reader.

Can one be "stuck" spiritually? I don't think so. We are justified. We are being sanctified and that is promised. None of that is our work, but all of it is God's. And yet, sometimes I don't see it. I lack the vision. Sometimes I don't understand what God is doing or asking me to do.

This type of blindness is different from lacking faith. In faith, we understand there is something there that we are sure of that we cannot see. This is not the same as wanting knowledge that is outside of our limitations, like in the garden of Eden, when Adam and Eve wanted to be independent and free of their need for God. No, this is a yearning in us, put there by the Holy Spirit, to want to understand something, and yet, being aware that we can't see what we should be able to see, even if we aren't sure what that is. To put it plainly, this is a place of being at the end of our ropes. It's the tension of being to be out of ideas, combined with a sense of pressing urgency.

> "God, I don't know what to do. I don't know which direction to go. I have run out of ideas. I don't know how to respond. I don't know my next step. I can't see."

During these times of intense stress, there are not many who have the option to go quietly into a cabin in the woods and have a prayer retreat to seek wisdom from the Lord. No, if anything, the opportunities to seek the Lord feel reduced in these seasons. Either your marriage seems to be crumbling, or the child's heart is out of reach, or that person who was your rock has died, or something about your vocation is crushing you, and nothing seems to be helping.

You pray. You read your Bible. You try to meditate, but worries of the situation start to swirl in your brain as demands from those around you increase. You're stuck.

This is where I wish we did more training on fasting, because the Bible mentions it in nineteen places in just the Old Testament alone.[2] For those counting, the Scriptures mention it a lot more than Bible journaling.

The New Testament mentions fasting fifteen times, but only in a narrative sense, in the four gospels and in Acts. Fasting isn't mentioned in the epistles to the church by means of instruction. The church just did it. It was culturally normal. It is no longer culturally normal, at least where I live in middle-class America, unless it's combined with shakes and a work-out routine. I don't know if Jesus and the early church fasted while drinking protein shakes and doing work-out routines, but I see no evidence of it in the text.

It's important that we understand the context of fasting with a firm view of sound theology, otherwise we will slip into gnostic beliefs that we must kill the body to make way for spiritual life. That is not what the Bible means when it talks about "the flesh." The flesh refers to our sinful desires, not our physical body. Jesus Christ was completely God and completely human. In his presence, he healed people's hearts, as well as their bodies. He valued both. Fasting in a way that harms your body is not biblical.

Each one of us has such a unique body. Mine is small and has always been small. I never reached desirable marks on growth charts as a child. Doctors were always poking me with needles and weighing me with concern, trying to figure out why I didn't fit on a chart. If my husband and I go to a restaurant, and I order a glass of wine, I usually only drink about half of it. I'm just a small thing, and my body can't handle more.

On the other hand, my husband is a big guy. He played high school and college football, and he now farms full time, working a lot with his hands. He has a strong handshake and broad shoulders. No one has ever called him tiny. At the restaurant, he can have a couple of beers, and not even feel tingly.

If the Bible were to give instructions on how much alcohol is appropriate, would it be more reasonable to say, "do not get drunk" or would it be more reasonable to say "not more than 8 oz of 10% proof alcohol." The Bible warns against drunkenness, but it does not forbid drinking; in fact, drinking alcohol is mentioned in a positive light numerous times in Scripture.

Similarly, we won't find specifics for fasting. While drinking can gladden the heart and is mode for celebration, fasting is for humbling and what a beautiful humbling it is.

We often equate humbling with humiliating, and but there is no shame in this humbling. There is only reality. Rather than pushing our limits, through fasting, we openly admit them to God, assuming a humble position to our prayers. "I simply don't understand. I am unable. I am helpless without you."

Fasting is an act of stepping into the power of God, when our souls need evidence of his sufficiency. It is not receiving the power to wield as we choose. Fasting often brings clarity or peace. It is a wonderful gift to exercise when all of our coping skills are no longer effective.

Rules about fasting are extremely limited in the Bible. So, the specifics of fasting won't help you. The rules are not the road to holiness. Fasting does not cast a spell. Freedom abounds so that this spiritual discipline might be applied particularly.

What do you depend on instead of God?

If attention is the basis of prayer, fasting is hyper-focused attention for those who do not have the means to give it. Most of us seek not only nourishment, but comfort from food. When we go to food for comfort, and it is not there, our minds start their frantic search as to why. We get unsettled and antsy. To be honest, I have the same reaction these days when I'm away from my phone. When we restrict this comfort, it has a two-fold purpose: to remind our minds to pray, and to teach us that comfort is found in more than our usual.

Abstaining from Nourishment vs Abstaining from Comfort

The goal is not to beat your body, starve it, or bring it into submission. If you have a history of eating disorders, fast from something other than food, like an alcoholic might drink grape juice instead of wine at communion. It is wise to be aware of our weaknesses, so that we do not tempt Satan. You have nothing to prove. You are secure in Christ.

We all have our coping mechanisms, those things we run to when we start to feel stress. Do we run to food, to our smartphones, to a person, to social media, to the television? Do we run to something other than God? Fasting is a means of discipline that removes our knee-jerk coping mechanisms so that when we start to feel the urge to reach for that thing, we reach to God instead. We are human, and we cannot sustain a fast of something good God has given us to use, nor should we. But we should have the freedom to understand that God is the one who is sustaining us, not these things that grab our attention, or we miss when they're gone.

The modern Western culture does not fit with fasting. Where I live, it's something that Catholics and liturgical Protestants associate with Lent. Here in the West, we don't have the traditional knowledge in our churches anymore about fasting. You don't hear much of people doing it. We don't know why you would do it, besides perhaps to lose some weight. Fasting seems to have nothing to do with our spiritual lives.

I used to resist the idea of fasting because, to me, it looks like a spiritual temper tantrum. A hunger strike until God does what you want. Other times, I'd heard of it as a supercharger that we attach to prayers to make them go farther. Does God work even like that?

My first encounter with someone actually fasting was when I was on a short-term mission trip in the Philippines when I was 15 years old. There was a local pastor at a church where we were staying. I was talking to the pastor one day in his office, with several other students, and I noticed on his schedule, he had written on every Thursday "Fasting and prayer." I asked him, "Do you really fast every Thursday? Why would you do that?"

He looked at me and smiled. He said through his thick accent, "This neighborhood, where we live, there is much evil. The spiritual warfare is great. The forces against the gospel being spread are great. I have to fast every week so that I can remember in my suffering: the suffering of Christ. It helps me to remember that it is by Christ's suffering, not me being busy and following every need in the village, that there is victory. It takes my eyes off my works and puts them on Christ's strength. That remembrance gives my ministry power."

His actions didn't give him power. Showing off his holy works didn't give him power. Admitting his tendency to take on the whole burden of ministry on his own shoulders and submitting to weekly humbling as a means to remember where power did come from gave him power.

> "In the biblical context, however, fasting carries a different meaning [than a hunger strike]. It is not a way of asserting one's will but a means of opening oneself to the work of God, expressing profound grief over sin and pointing to one's ultimate dependence on God for all forms of sustenance."[3]

Spiritual fasting isn't a diet. You don't fast from something that's bad for you, like cigarettes. You give up something that's good, like food, for the purpose of awakening your soul to your desperate state. Generally, the idols in our lives aren't something that appear evil. They are things that appear good, and because they are good, we wrongly worship them instead of God. It's not performing, not losing a few pounds, not manipulating. It's allowing yourself to be uncomfortable because God can show us some amazing things when we are honest about our desperate need for him.

Fasting in Community

I used to fast with my roommate when I was in college, as we went on prayer walks around the city on our fasting days. Twenty years and six children later, I found that I wasn't practicing fasting at all anymore. I knew I shouldn't fast from food when I was pregnant and nursing, which for me lasted years. I did pray, though. After all, prayer isn't a manipulation of God either, but a communion with God. But I wondered why I didn't fast, when it's mentioned so often with prayer. What was my prejudice against it? As I pondered this question, I entered into a season with one of my kids that I wasn't handling well. This child was being mouthy to me, rude to her siblings, and as she was working through her anger towards a hard situation, she was disrupting any peace in our home. Discipline wasn't working. Time with her one-on-one wasn't working. Every intervention wasn't helping. Prayer didn't even feel like it was working.

Since I started studying fasting just before this season, I decided to just do it. I should stop reading about it, and just fast, I decided. I decided to fast for a full day, using any discomfort I was in as a prompt to pray for this child. I was desperate to try anything. I didn't have much expectation of what God was going to do—more of a curiosity.

It was difficult. I have broken fasts before by accident, and God never smote me for it. But this day I actually completed it. That day I had my personal weaknesses right in front of my face the entire time. I felt annoyed, but quiet. I did not feel proud of myself for completing the fast, I felt more aware of my frailty than ever. My need for God was evident the whole day. My resolve that my daughter was only going to get through this season by the grace of God was fixed. The whole exercise was God helping me to fix my eyes on his salvation. It helped me understand that it was ok to say I wasn't enough, ok to say I didn't know what to do, ok to say, "Jesus, by your salvation alone will this be resolved."

My daughter was wonderful that day. Part of it, I think, is that the Holy Spirit kept my mouth shut a lot. My whole attitude towards her changed as compassion grew. She got a lot off her chest, and it was almost as if the Holy Spirit would not let me open my mouth to counter her arguments. Just listen. It was a respite from our weeks of fighting.

The next morning, I sat down to a hearty breakfast. I took one bite and she walked into the kitchen and bitterness came out of her mouth towards me as I chewed. I felt more than defeated. I texted my aunt and mentor who first got me thinking about this "fasting experiment." I told her, "Yesterday was amazing. Hard, but good. This morning I'm eating breakfast, I haven't even said a word to her, and the awfulness is back. I cannot fast every day. I'm going to die."

She texted back, "I haven't eaten yet today. I'll fast for you today. You eat and be replenished."

"I'll fast for you."

Those words on the screen hit me. She would do that? For me and my daughter? She would fast for me? It's one thing to say that you'll pray for someone. That takes just a few seconds. But fasting in my place? That's willingly suffering for someone. She wasn't even in the situation. The Holy Spirit didn't need to train her to shut my mouth and listen as he needed to with mine.

I ate that day, but I continued praying and meditating on the idea of willingly suffering for another. My mind kept thinking of my aunt, and the ministry of sharing in sufferings for each other. Her fasting, maybe even more than mine, pointed me to the ministry of Christ, suffering in our place. We can't fast every day. We would die.

That fast was not a work I completed to God. It was actually a rest God gave me. A rest of trying to be the perfect mom, of trying to say the right thing, from trying to address every issue in the best way. It was a day of me saying "God, when I am weak, you are strong. Help me."

Fasting isn't something we have to do for God. It's a gift God has given us, when we need to understand that our weakness isn't something we need to fear, because of his strength on the cross.

CHAPTER 12

Confession

"Therefore when I admonish you to confession
I am admonishing you to be a Christian."

—MARTIN LUTHER
LARGE CATECHISM[1]

AFTER MY PARENTS' DIVORCE when I was 5, our church decided
to do some intense conflict resolution training for all ages. We
watched videos Sunday nights, and learned how to give an apology—
including all the parts and stages that go along with that, how to
accept an apology, and rebuild trust. The formula for a full apology
was laid out and dissected for us to see all of the parts, and what
each part does. The lessons I learned from there have stuck with
me, and I've been so intentional to teach my kids how to give a full
apology well. For instance, say "I" statements, not "you" statements.
"I lied" not "you made me lie." Also, you can't twist it to a "you" statement by saying things like "I'm sorry you took it the wrong way." We
learned about setting healthy boundaries and making sure we are
fighting fair.

Later in life, and in my own marriage, my very stoic husband was
taught that it wasn't as much about saying you're sorry as much as
it was to actually be sorry. Talk doesn't mean as much as changed

actions. Once you realize you did something wrong, turn and stop doing it. That's what repentance is. When he makes a mistake, he will usually beat himself up internally and without a word, he tries harder. Many of our arguments are about me saying that I actually need to hear the words, not just assume he is thinking them. I'm annoying in my pursuit of covering technicalities.

He is getting better at saying "I'm sorry." I'm getting better at just forgiving him.

There is a tug and pull between "talk is cheap" and only actions matter, and then on the other side, words having the capacity to build someone up or tear them down. Words have power.

What comes first, grace or repentance? In an effort to teach our kids law and gospel theology, I have expressed to them many times that they do not need to fear because whenever they say they are sorry, they will always be forgiven. It's been a little more difficult to define forgiveness, as sometimes there are consequences, but our relationship will always be intact. We will always love them. We will always be willing to work with them to rebuild trust.

More times than I can count, a child will be adamantly defending what they did that was wrong, and as I'm pointing out the folly of their argument, they switch gears and say "I'm sorry, ok?!? Are you happy now? I'm sorry. Now you have to stop telling me I'm wrong." I try to explain that just because we will always forgive them when they say they are sorry, the words "I'm sorry" isn't a giant "shut up now" button you can just press. God will not be mocked.

To admit you are wrong is painful. The full understanding of the weight of your sin dawns on you. It often floods us with shame—but that shame is not from God. The Holy Spirit convicts us, but he does not condemn us. Satan will take our shame and condemn us, cancel us, and attach it to our identities. He will use our sin to name us. The fear of him doing so is why confessing sin is so terrifying.

But when we confess to our God, he removes that sin from us. He gives us his family name, his identity. He is not asking us to prove it, and any act of proving is for our understanding of the depth of this truth, not his. He doesn't need things proven to him. He knows our hearts better than we know them (1 John 3:20).

If you are sorry, and you say sorry, do you automatically stop sinning? Usually not. Unfortunately, until our glorification, we will still struggle with sin. Therefore, confession is and should be a regular part of the Christian life. The reason for this isn't that we need to be re-saved, or re-forgiven, or that every time we sin, we are in mortal danger of losing our salvation. The reason for this is that sin festers, and Satan accuses. Confession and absolution are active reminders that God's grace remains. It is an active encouragement that goes to the deepest and most intimate parts of our lives. When we say "you are forgiven" we aren't saying anything that the gospel hasn't already done.

The Misuse of Confession

While volumes have been written on conflict resolution, this chapter is actually on the spiritual discipline of confession. That is different from conflict resolution, although it sometimes takes place during a conflict. The outcome of confession is often reconciliation with peers, but not always. Confession is not a guarantee that everything will turn out alright, and you'll have no consequences. My children sometimes shout at me "I'm sorry!!" as I'm pointing out to them something they

---

did wrong, but "sorry" is not a magic word for "stop talking about it already" that you can pull out to silence someone. You cannot silence a victim of your sin with an "I'm sorry."

Healing sometimes takes time. Love is patient. God is patient. Too many times I see that someone says, "I'm sorry" and immediately goes into offense mode of "he/she hasn't forgiven me yet. They need to repent of unforgiveness. They're keeping a record of wrong." (This concept is covered even more in depth in the chapter on lament.)

Say you are backing up your car, and you accidentally (or even purposefully) run over your friend's foot as you are backing up. The foot is broken. You immediately see your wrongdoing and you say "I'm sorry! I'm so sorry!"

Your friend is generous. She says, "of course I forgive you!" Would you then say, "I don't know why you're going to the hospital for x-rays. I think you're just preparing for a lawsuit against me. I think you're trying to keep records of my wrong." Your friend will say, "but my foot is broken." Every time she says that, you say, "stop throwing it in my face already! You said I was forgiven. You won't stop bringing it up!" Your friend may heal eventually. The injury may fester from time to time. Of course, this injury can be brought up in manipulating ways, but commenting on the reality of it isn't unforgiveness. It's just the reality of her brokenness.

We may say that when someone hurts someone else, the person who sinned is responsible to fix it, but that is not always possible. If you broke my foot, I don't want you to set my foot, I want a doctor to do that. In a marriage, if someone has been abusive, the abuser can't be the one to fix it, it will usually be a counselor, police, or social worker of some sort. This is where vocation comes into play. When we forgive someone, we acknowledge that God will direct the healing, and God will use the vocations of others to help with that process. There have been so many times that I have expected someone who sinned against me to fix the hurt, and that doesn't always work *because they are broken too*. According to civil law, people may be responsible to pay for help, or pay for repairs. God is certainly not against justice. But we need to think more broadly when we are trying to heal, meaning we cannot always look to the perpetrator to be the healer.

In forgiveness, we remember: they are broken sinners in need of grace too. Do not put them in the place of the Savior to heal your hurt.

We do the same thing spiritually and emotionally. We apologize to people and expect them to not be broken anymore. We shame them with being "unforgiving" for dealing with the reality of the pain we have inflicted upon them. This is not true confession.

Confession isn't for our manipulative use. Confession doesn't keep us from consequences here on earth. If you confessed a murder to the police, I'm guessing they wouldn't say, "Well, as long as you're sorry . . ." Confessions aren't a guarantee for reconciliation with others.

You can't say, "Yes, I punched you. But now that I've apologized, you must accept and aren't allowed to leave me." Or "Yes, I lied to you over and over, but now that I confessed, you must believe me, or you are unforgiving."

So, what are confession and absolution, and why are we called to practice them? Like all the other spiritual disciplines, they are tools intended to center us to the reality of Jesus' death on the cross and his resurrection.

How Confession Benefits an Individual

When we confess, we confess both positive and negative things. For instance, we confess the Apostle's Creed. We are to confess what we believe. Say what is true. This is where I stand. Call them ancient affirmations about God, the practice of confessing what you know to be true, especially when it doesn't always feel true. Though they distinguish themselves from affirmations in the sense that they are not about self, as much as they are about truth. Speak what is true. Hold to what is true. Confessing the creeds often feels like an act of defiance against the enemy for me. To confess what is true is encouraging, empowering, and can beat back feelings that do not align with the truth when doubt creeps in.

We also confess negative things, mainly our sin. While traditional modern affirmations speak hopeful sayings of strength and power over ourselves, Christian confession speaks of the strength of our God, and the weakness in ourselves. We confess our sin, because it is also true.

> "If we confess our sin, he is faithful and just to forgive our sin, and cleanse us from all unrighteousness." (1 John 1:9)

Confession is the opposite of pretending. It's the opposite of faking it until you make it and hoping no one notices. Confession is rooting yourself in truth. This is who God is. This is what I did, and it is against what God calls good.

We can confess in private to God, and he will accept it. Confessing doesn't mean "making public." There are times when it is good and right to keep a small circle. There are other times when public confession is good and right, especially in cases when doing so will protect others. However, confessing, I believe, is most beautiful when you have someone to confess to. There is healing when you confess to someone else, even if it's not the person you offended. Why? Because when you have sinned, the most comforting thing you can hear is an absolution. Faith is built when we hear the word of Christ.

How Confession Benefits the Community of Believers

"In confession the break-through to community takes place. Sin demands to have man by himself. It withdraws him from the community. The more isolated a person is, the more destructive will be the power of sin over him and the more deeply he becomes involved in it, the more disastrous is his isolation. Sin wants to remain unknown. It shuns the light."[2]

Before the reformation, absolution was considered something that only priests had the authority to do. People would confess, and you were given penance to make up for your sin. One of the major theologies of the Reformation is the priesthood of all believers. That means that if you believe in Christ, you can absolve people, which means you get to tell people that Jesus died for their sins.

This is when sound doctrine enters our friendships between believers. Between friends, it can sometimes be difficult to know how to respond when someone is confessing. Sometimes we don't even realize they are confessing. They're just talking about the difficulties of their day. Our friend will talk about their day. They will list the things that they wish they had not done. "And then I really lost my temper. I just hate myself. Ugh. I don't know what to do." There are two common responses to exclamations like this, and they are both wrong.

The first common response is "You know, we all do it. It's okay." We are trying to make our friend feel better. But was it okay? Just because we all do it, does it make it right, or does it make it common? Downplaying sin isn't helpful. We are all trying to believe it, but really it just silences the hurt and shame that comes from sinning. It doesn't remove it—it just hides it.

The second common response is "Wow, you're really messed up. You actually did that? You need to get some help. Like some serious help. What's the matter with you?" This is known as giving someone the "law." This is different from telling an alcoholic that you will help them get help, something that is usually done with compassion. This is giving someone the law in order to shame them. Offering help is loving, and it is often needed. Shaming them for their sin is not.

One of the purposes of the law is to show us our need for the gospel. The purpose of the law is to show us our need for Christ. When the law is given without the gospel of Christ, we are basically handing out death (2 Cor. 7:10).

The absolving answer—the answer that points them to Christ is: "For this sin Christ died. Do you know that? God loved you so deeply that he sent his son to rescue you from this sin. You mean that much to him. This sin is no joke, but he is bigger. He is for you."

Such an answer does not diminish the sin. It does not shame. It absolves. Giving absolution is fun and addicting, because we can give it freely and lavishly. It's a message that God wants us to spread far and wide. It catches people off balance. It stops people in their self-shaming and points them to the love of God. It stops people from downplaying sin and points them to the redeeming love of Jesus.

Rooting Out Anti-Confession

We have a habit in our family that I have been slowly trying to break. The theology of a weighted scale creeps into our defense of ourselves. When we go to a brother or sister, husband or wife, and say "what you did hurt me." The response should be "I'm sorry. Please forgive me."

But instead, the knee jerk reaction is, "why are you upset with me when I've done all of these other good things! Don't you notice all the good things I've done? Do those even count for anything?" Every person in my house does this, including me. I work hard to encourage, notice the good things, compliment, and build up. Also, it's not wise to constantly point out other people's sin. The Holy Spirit directs hearts, and especially for those who are parents, we must learn to choose our battles, so we don't exasperate us all. But when something is wrong, it is wrong, and the good things we did don't cancel out that wrong.

We do that with God too, don't we? "But don't you notice the good things I do? Shouldn't that count for something?" I explain to my kids that this is actually an Islamic belief in a weighted scale, where the argument you are presenting is that your good deeds outweigh your bad deeds. "In this house," I say "We don't believe in weighing our good deeds against our bad deeds. We believe in bringing our bad deeds to Christ for forgiveness. And his forgiveness is always guaranteed. There's no need to be afraid."

In order to do this, we have to call a sin a sin. This seems to be the most painful part of it, and it is where we have the most resistance. We feel justified in our sin. We feel we had a right to sin. We feel our sin wasn't *that bad*. Calling it "bad" or "sin" without a qualifier as to the degree just feels harsh. We humans hate letting go of our self-justifications with everything in us.

- I was provoked.
- She deserved it.
- I deserve this bad "indulgence."
- I'm just doing my thing.
- I wasn't *trying* to be mean.
- It's not as bad as what he did.
- He did it first.
- "The woman whom you gave to be with me, she gave me the fruit of the tree . . ."
- "The serpent deceived me . . ."

We justify our sin, and it does us no good. We must let go of our self-justifications and embrace Christ's justification.

Confession gets to the truth of who we are, what we did, who God is, and what he did.

Throughout church history, the church has not always had a good handle on this in practice. If you've ever heard about a church scandal, the root of it is that someone, at some point believed one of two lies. They either thought that some sin wasn't so bad, or that it was so bad that confessing it would do damage to the church.

All sin needs the forgiveness of Christ. There is no degree where it's fine, and we don't have to worry about it. Also, if the purpose of church is to make disciples and teach them about the forgiveness of sins. So, if we were to say that some sins are too big to confess, we would undermine the communication of the power of the very gospel we are called to preach. Church scandals are so heartbreaking because it isn't just about the ugliness of the sin. It's the complete abandonment of either the need for the gospel or of the proclamation of the power of the gospel.

For this sin Jesus died, that you may be forgiven. Feel the weight of that love. Feel the weight of how seriously God takes sin. He does not qualify it. He will not allow us to justify it. The only thing we have in our power to do is to confess it. By confessing it, we speak truth over the lie we believed when we sinned in the first place. When we confess the truth of the sin, we stop the lie in its tracks.

"You are forgiven" are the most powerful words that can be spoken. And by some great mercy, God has not only allowed us, but has called us to speak those powerful words over others on his behalf.

• CHAPTER 13 •

Generosity

"the Spirit and the gifts are ours
through him who with us sideth.
Let goods and kindred go,
this mortal life also;
the body they may kill:
God's truth abideth still;
his kingdom is forever!"

—MARTIN LUTHER
A MIGHTY FORTRESS IS OUR GOD

NOTHING BRINGS OUT OUR politics, worldviews, and deep-seated beliefs like when we talk about our money, or our time, or our possessions. We go down rabbit trails, like the best form of government to care for the poor, which is most biblical, and when helping hurts. Can we help "too much?" Can we give "too much?"

In the world of extremes, we can either feel like poor people bring their situation upon themselves and have nothing to do with us, or like an acquaintance of mine from years ago, he gave away so much he had to file for bankruptcy. He was giving away money that he didn't even have.

So then, is the solution moderation? The problem with moderation, or riding the middle line, is that it depends so completely on our feelings and our points of view. This feels like an appropriate thing to do. This is enough, without going too far.

Once again, we bring back into our vocabulary the word "enough" and ask ourselves if we are doing it. Like any other part of the Christian life, it is Christ who is enough. He has given us his Spirit to show us. When we think that it is our emotions that guide us, it only reveals how shallow our understanding of the Holy Spirit actually is.

Generosity is not something that we accomplish or check off. We don't tithe and consider it done. It is a matter of the heart that the Holy Spirit is continually sanctifying. There are several areas of generosity: financial giving, of course, but there's also giving time. Generosity also relates to hospitality. When you are at a party, do you try to find the most interesting person, or do you seek out the one who is excluded? Generosity of heart has as much to do with picking up a check at a restaurant as it does with forgiving someone who doesn't deserve it. With everything God has given you, be generous. Be generous with how you respond to the person on the internet. Be generous with your toddler who is always tired.

Generosity in actions only leads to superiority or manipulative martyrdom, which both lead to exhaustion, because we will never get the credit we feel we should receive for being "technically" generous. Generosity is a gift to us and to our hearts because it roots us in reminders of the generosity and sufficiency of Christ.

The Act of Lifting Others Up

My grandpa was one of the most generous people I know, and he was probably one of the poorest. He worked in missions and church planting at a time when pastors really didn't save for retirement. He had a knack for flipping houses, so they lived off of that income in their later years. But when I say he was generous, I don't mean he gave people lots of money, though I'd never known him to not fight for the check at a restaurant.

When my grandpa or any of his siblings came into a room full of relatives at a family reunion, they would go straight for the children and look them each in the eye and tell them how precious they were and how much Jesus loved them. They always started with the children. "Because they're the most important," my grandpa would say. He taught me through example to always sit at the least important part of a table at a holiday, not because I wanted to be asked to the head of the table, but because the lowest spot was actually where the "real" treasure was.

One of the things many of his dependents remember about his generosity, though, was his generous apologies. When he apologized, he did so without any "buts." His apologies were never, ever qualified or lessened. He never made you feel ashamed for being mad, or struggling to forgive, or just needing time. He just would take whatever blame he could. It was almost as if the shame of being in the wrong couldn't touch him, so he took as much blame as possible. He would be generous with his restitution. It was like he had a secret stash of grace, so that he could take whatever blame upon himself and not be crushed, because he had the antidote easily at his disposal. He wasn't flippant. He was just that convinced of God's grace for him, that he literally had nothing to lose.

When we went to his house, there were always treats. He gave bear hugs. He looked people in the eye and made them feel honored. I will not let the discussion of "generosity" fall into the mostly monetary category. The most generous man I knew was also the poorest.

Experiencing the Lavishness of Grace

The concept of "too much grace" gets brought up when we bring up the idea of generosity. Grace is lavish. The concept of excessive grace stems from a weak view of the law. We think the law is doable, so others should do it like we are doing it. When we understand that one of the purposes of the law is to show us our sin, we will understand the need for grace. When we think the law is obtainable, we think grace is excessive. If we only understood how weak and broken by sin the human race is, grace would no longer seem excessive. We would see it as perfectly necessary.

> "See what kind of love the Father has given to us, that we should be called children of God; and so we are. The reason why the world does not know us is that it did not know him." (1 John 3:1)

Generosity turns from gospel to law when we see ourselves as the only beneficiaries. For example, saying that we tithe so that we may be blessed. Do this so you can get that. Generosity, when Holy Spirit driven, is incredibly humbling. It has us thinking: "I can't believe I get to do this. I can't believe that God would let me be a part of this ministry in this way." When we understand that it was God who created everything that is, that he spoke it into being, that he sent his son to live a perfect life and die for us—God is incredibly capable. He does not need us. He chooses to involve us, because it is good. He chooses to involve us to consistently point to our redemption. Generosity is good for our hearts, when we lay down something we see as part of our life, for someone else.

There is a contentment expressed in generosity. I have everything I need. I don't need honor, I don't need money or approval. I have Jesus. And my work, my joy, is to distribute his love as lavishly as I want without running out.

There's a scene in the movie "The Incredibles" which my children have watched more times than I can count. The boy in that movie is "Dash" and his whole life he has had to hide his superpowers. His superpower is his speed. He can run so fast that no one can see him. Besides using his superpower to torment his teachers, he never got to express what was put in him. But when his family was in trouble, his parents told him to run as fast as he could. The bad guys were after him, and he ran faster than he ever did before. As he did so, he started running on water. When he realized what he was doing, he looked down at his feet and gave a deep throated giggle. His gifts could now be truly expressed in him, and it felt good.

Our gifts are not our wages for our work. The development of our gifts stem from the bottomless inheritance of grace we have been given. When the Holy Spirit calls us to give generously, whether of our money, time, status, or with our words and actions, we might step into the calling with hesitation, as though we are doing something that we have been taught not to do. We know we aren't breaking God's laws, but we are breaking the world's normal expectations. The world has told us that people will take advantage of us, that it's every man for himself. Generosity isn't what regular people do. Through generosity, we are tapping into something more powerful than the world offers. When you start to feel the power of grace in generosity, you can't help but give a deep throated giggle like Dash running on water. That was fun. I didn't know it was like that. Let's do it again.

Generosity isn't natural. It's supernatural. That's what makes it so fun. It's not playing by the rules of the world.

The Story of the Two Sons

In Luke 15 Jesus tells the story about two sons. The younger son asks for his inheritance while his father still lives, and then squanders it through sinful living. When he is at the brink of starvation, he returns to his father. He offers to be a servant just to get fed, and his father takes him back with open arms and restores him. He runs out to meet him. He hugs him. He gives him the best clothes, honors, and food. He wanted to show him the depth of his love.

The older son heard the party celebrating his younger brother's return, and he refused to go. The father came out to meet him as well and invited him in to celebrate. What happened during that conversation is heartbreaking, as the heart of the older brother is exposed. He feels he has a right to his father's riches, not because he is a son, but because of his works. He wants his works to count for something. He values his own achievements and merits over his father's love and generosity.

The father, says in almost a heartbroken way: "Did you not know that all I have is yours?"

You don't give to earn favor with God. God has given you meaningful work because you are in his family, but he doesn't show favoritism among his children. Sometimes that feels unfair. We feel God should show favoritism, at least for the people who are more gifted or work harder. We forget that our gifts and work ethic come from God, and they are a part of the gifts given to us in grace, not a part of our works.

Our gifts and ability are for the glory of God. We just wish we could keep the glory. We feel entitled to it.

The core of the older brother's anger wasn't his younger brother's good fortune of having a forgiving, generous father. That was just the spark that ignited the dry fuel within him. It was the fact that the older brother viewed his inheritance as wages. He thought he had properly earned them. His father told him that everything he had was simply given to him for the fact that he was his son. The father had not even taken into consideration how hard the older son had worked when he had lavished his inheritance on him. The older son would have preferred wages for his work to an inheritance. He wanted to earn it. He saw the money as rightfully his, by his own hard work. Acknowledging that it was all a gift robbed him of his autonomy and made it about his father's generosity rather than about his work ethic.

And if it was all about the father's generosity, then the older son was no better than his younger brother. That means his father loved them the same, and the older brother couldn't handle that.

At the core of our resistance to generosity is the belief that we earned this. This belongs to me. This wasn't given to me by my father, this was something I earned with my own two hands.

The father didn't mind the older son working for him. He enjoyed it. It was how they spent time together. It's how they bonded, and where he passed on all the knowledge he had to give. To the father, his son working for him was evidence that he was his son. Everything he had, he gave to his son. Why should he not enjoy the pleasure of working and developing what belongs to him?

How do you view your work—your vocation? Is it a gift that God has given you, as you do the good works he has prepared for you to do for the benefit of others? Or is it something that you do to get what you want? Having money is not evil. However, seeing that money as something you earned through your own power and wisdom will make you miserly and stingy.

When you see your wealth as a result of your abilities and don't recognize that your abilities are a pure gift from God, you are living in an illusion.

At its core, the issue isn't about our money. The issue is rooted out through the call to generosity. The issue is us gripping our own works and rights in every area of our lives, because we feel we are above the generous grace of God.

It's not that wealth of any kind is bad, or that God is out to make you poor (though there is no shame in being poor). The reason God works on this part of our hearts is that grace is more valuable. The gold of grace makes our works look like rags. Grace is more abundant. Grace is the true riches. His heart is to break the illusion and for us to know the truth.

The older son had no idea how to enjoy his riches. The father knew that the greatest joy came from giving the riches away. He was trying to teach his son how to use his inheritance, but that was impossible to do as long as the son saw them as his wages from his work. This is mine. I earned it. None of this was given to me. It's all me. The arrogance of such a thought! To tell the father that gave you life, who gave you riches, and gave you meaningful work, that nothing of yours is a gift, but a result of your own effort? His blindness kept him not only from understanding, but from joy.

Our Works Get in the Way,
Suffering Brings Understanding

One of the reasons why money comes into play so often in the topic of giving is that "our money" is the greatest symbol of our works that we have. When it comes to money, every human will claim they are entitled to it. We earned this. We did this. This is all mine. The reason why it's so important to be generous with money is because it loosens this idea in us that it is ours and belongs to us. There is no job we've ever had that God did not give us. There is no work we have done that he didn't prepare in advance for us to do. Money is where our faith that we are saved by grace hits reality. It's all grace.

Love from God is abundant and active. It cannot be dammed and held back. Letting love run through us to others is often God's greatest gift to us. That does not mean it is without pain. In fact, very often our suffering and exhaustion is an asset to us as we try to understand generosity. The younger brother knew the depths from which he was saved. He understood the love of the father better. He understood better that his inheritance wasn't wages. Through humility, he plunged into the depths of his father's love.

The most generous people I know have the greatest understanding of suffering. They have the greatest understanding of the toll that exhaustion takes. Because of their pain, they have compassion. Let that thought sink in for a moment. Generosity doesn't have as much to do with how much we own, how much we are capable of giving, or how much time we have. It has to do with our understanding of suffering. It has to do with our understanding of our depravity, and the rich grace that is at our disposal to distribute.

God understands our suffering better than anyone (Heb. 4:15). His generosity of grace lavished upon people who cannot help themselves comes from his depth of understanding our suffering.

Participating in the generosity of God is a gift, and it doesn't come from God's lack or his need for our help. When it is a rightly understood sign of our restoration, not a condition to our restoration, there is no need to resist it. Every step of generosity will help us understand the generous nature of our Father. When we give under compulsion, we become the martyr. We feel the exhaustion, *because it will never be enough*. But when we give just for the fun of it, just to feel God's love flow through us, like Dash discovering he can run on water, we feel the rush of power that love gives, as we feel the enormity of it, the force of it, and we grow in the depth of the knowledge that it will never, ever run dry.

CHAPTER 14

Lament

"No one ever told me that grief felt so like fear.
I am not afraid, but the sensation is like being afraid."

—C.S. LEWIS
A GRIEF OBSERVED[1]

I WOKE UP THAT morning in tears. I couldn't figure out what was with me the last few days. I wasn't overtired. I wasn't hormonal. I was on the edge of tears pretty much all day for days. I was snapping and exploding at my husband for minor things. My temper touched my chronic pain, and I fell into a scary migraine. I would fall apart as a spiral of grief. I would remember that event, then that other event, then pain from my past, like threads of grief that were all hanging loose would hang down around me, and I would emotionally spin, touching the end of each strand.

What was going on? Am I literally going crazy? Is this physical, psychological, spiritual, or what?

I looked at my calendar as I was preparing a grocery list and saw the anniversary of some deeply painful incidents on the horizon. What should I make for supper on that evening, when I'm trying to forget that rejection, one of my deepest hurts?

ᅟ

As I emotionally spiraled, touching the threads of pain that were tangling my heart, my husband urged me that I have to get over some of this. I have to learn how to let go. This grief is strangling me. I agreed. I nodded with tears in my eyes. There's nothing I want more than to let go. But . . . how do I make this hurting stop?

We are holistic creatures. There are physical things we can do to help grief. There are physical elements to anxiety, depression, and pain. We sometimes need medications or help. We sometimes need exercise. Counseling can equip us to think clearly, and a good friend—how can you even put a value on such a treasure? Sometimes I think that the reason that all of these "helps" help is because they are honest about the fact that there is a problem.

"Sometimes it feels like there's no grace leftover for me." I tell my husband. I'm ashamed of my grief. The poet Rachel Joy Welcher writes "I feel like my brokenness is breaking everything."[2] I want to push past the lament. I see how it affects my family. I feel like I'm burdening those around me, and above all else, I don't want to be the problem-person. I don't want burdening others to be my legacy.

Lament is humbling, which is why it's often connected with fasting. We cannot look away from the truth that we need saving. We cannot pretend any longer. We cannot go forward without help. The breath of God still fills our lungs as we breathe in and breathe out.

I don't want to be the person who always needs help, the downer, the super-sensitive one. It's bad enough to know that you're too sensitive, or you're going through a tough season. It's hard when others are sad from just being around you. It's hard enough being low. I don't want to bring others down with me. I don't want to be the weakest link.

Like the other disciplines, mourning or lament have both an individual and communal aspect to them. We must learn to both mourn, and to mourn with others. It is individual because no one can mourn for you. It cannot be delegated. You must walk through it as an individual. Avoiding it just delays it and usually makes a monster of it. It's communal because we are not to mourn alone. When one part of the body hurts, the whole body hurts. God tells us to mourn with those who mourn—not shame those who mourn—not dismiss those who mourn. Sit in the sadness.

I list mourning as a spiritual discipline because it is written about in depth in Scripture, and because mourning fits the liturgy of being made aware of our weakness and being pointed to the work of Jesus on the cross. Most don't think about mourning as a discipline because it greatly disrupts schedules, and we too often think of spiritual disciplines in terms of scheduling. There are no charts or planners for how to mourn. There is no checklist. There is no mourning-plan. No one sets a New Year's Resolution to mourn well that year. Because when we face a new year, we don't want to face that fact that we or someone we love may have to face death, or loss.

It is a discipline to submit to mourning, and it's a discipline to learn to mourn with others.

Mourning hits you at the worst times. When you arrive at a bridal shower, and something triggers a memory, and all of a sudden, you're crying and embarrassed. The last thing you want is to draw attention to yourself. This is not the place or time. *Get it together.*

"I will not be the problem person," you tell yourself. Pride drives the shame. When you realize that, you're ashamed of the pride too.

RAGGED

Developing the Heart of Patience

We are in a generation where it's not okay to not be okay. It's not okay to fail a test. It's not okay to make a mistake. Blame the "helicopter parents" or the "lawnmower parents" paving the way for their children to have a pain-free life. Those who say it's their chief goal for their children to "just be happy" soon realize that being happy all the time is quite a burden to put on a person. Being sad, or in a hard place means that you are somehow failing. Failing is unacceptable. We are afraid that failing at being happy gets classified as a mental disorder.

"Rejoice in hope, be patient in tribulation, be constant in prayer" (Rom. 12:12). The NIV translates "tribulation" as "affliction." What does it mean to be patient in affliction, and why is that paired up with joyfulness? The word patience means "long-suffering" or to put it another way, "a willingness to suffer."

Lament is a time when patience is developed by the Spirit. When you are lamenting, you will find people who will cheerfully hand you the formula to climb out of the pit and be happy. Then there are those who will climb in the pit with you, look into your eyes with understanding, and they will comfort you there. This is patience.

The willingness to suffer is not rushing someone through their pain for our own comfort. Patience is good because it's from the Spirit and reflects the very nature of God. If it were not for God's patience, he would have brought us home by now. But his will is that more people have the chance to hear of his salvation and believe. So he waits, as the world hurts.

How can joy and patience both be part of the fruit of the Spirit? James 1:2–4 might shine some understanding on it. "Count it all joy, my brothers, when you meet trials of various kinds, for you know that the testing of your faith produces steadfastness. And let steadfastness have its full effect, that you may be perfect and complete, lacking in nothing."

This doesn't mean we should command people mourning to have joy. Joy works its way in over time, as we see again and again what God accomplishes through trials. As friends of those who mourn, count it joy to be a part of their mourning, because you will see God at work. When someone meets us in our pain and stays with us, there is a hope that develops. There is an understanding that we are not alone no matter how much it hurts. This patience in lament shows the stability of love. There is nothing more hopeful or joyful than realizing God does not drop us when things get hard.

Unplanned Discipline

Lament is not always expected. It doesn't fit neatly on our calendars. It weaves in and out of our days, hitting us sometimes when we least expect it. I listed it as a spiritual discipline because a good portion of the Bible is about lament. Jesus himself mourned, therefore it is good. With all our ideals of things we do to understand God better, mourning somehow rarely makes the list. To be honest, most of us avoid mourning, and feel awkward around those who mourn. More than even fasting or other disciplines unusual in our culture, I believe we have lost the understanding of how God uses lament in our lives.

I mentioned in an earlier chapter my first real experience with mourning happened with an unexpected miscarriage. I had already had three children. Most people probably thought that should have been enough. I had never had trouble conceiving before. We were planning this child. Then one morning I started bleeding, and an ultrasound confirmed that the baby had died.

I felt totally unprepared for grief. No one told me how confusing it is. My brain was scanning, searching for a way to honor this life lost. In miscarriage especially, there is rarely a funeral or memorial service. What would I say? I lost something I barely knew, and yet it was most precious to me. No one told me how physically painful grief is. My whole body hurt, and not just from the physical elements of miscarriage.

Our lack of understanding of the value of lament is why we all say stupid things to those who are mourning. The strategy of the ignorant is to explain to the one mourning why they shouldn't feel pain.

- "The baby was probably very disabled, or not fully all there."
- "This is probably God saying you shouldn't have any more children."
- "God must have wanted another angel in heaven."
- "It's all for the best. It all works out for the good."

I'll never forget one of my pastors, upon finding out about our loss, coming up to me after the service, looking me right in the eyes and saying "This is an *enormous* loss. I'm so sorry you're grieving something so precious." Then he hugged me and caught a sob as his arms wrapped around me like a father comforting his child. He didn't tell me that I shouldn't be hurting. There was something healing about having my pain validated. It felt like it was honoring the value of what was lost.

Naming Things Correctly

Sometimes mourning or lamenting is the correct thing to do. It's how we recognize that something is wrong. When something is wrong, it would be wrong to pretend that it is alright. It's good to tell God something is wrong, instead of pretending it's fine. God calls us to "[Cast] all your anxieties upon him for he cares for you" (1 Pet. 5:7).

God doesn't consider you a problem person. He considers you a person.

Sometimes it feels like grieving is not looking to the work of Jesus enough, or not focusing on his resurrection and healing enough. Jesus rose from the dead! All is well! The longer the lament is ignored, the deeper its taproot anchors itself into the deepest parts of our lives. Someone dies. Someone is molested. Someone is chronically ill. Someone is rejected. Sin. Pain. Death. Grief. Lament.

Grief has a place in our spiritual life as a means of processing how God deals with sin. It is not only okay to say that something is wrong when it is wrong. It is good. It is truthful. It is honest.

Rarely is it convenient.

We do not have to seek out trials. They are promised to us. Perhaps Job responded to trials with "blessed be the name of the Lord" for a time, but there are later portions of that book where he demands an audience with God. The normalcy of trials does not lessen the pain. Stuffing the pain where no one can see it is just living a lie. Demanding others mourn with you is just flinging the pain around you. We must freely mourn with others, because it is good to sit in the truth of the pain, and to surround others as they are scanning for some way to deal with it, some avenue out, the ministry of saying, "you're not wrong. This does hurt. This is awful.

You're not making it up, and you're not doing it wrong," calms the grieving.

We see lament throughout the Psalms, Lamentations, and pretty much all of the prophets. We cry out as we live in the "already and not yet." Sometimes it's scary sitting in the cave waiting. We need to bring our pain to the light, where truth is revealed.

The Weight of Lament

There's nothing normal about death. There's nothing normal about sin. They don't belong in this world. God did not make them part of his design. Therefore, every time we bump into the brokenness of this world it stings. It's scary. The depth of the blackness and silence. Deep in our soul we know: this is not how it was supposed to be.

When God formed us out of dirt and breathed his own air into our lungs which caused our heart to start beating, the spark of life was put within us. God created life. He created us. We did not start out as sinners before the Fall. The world was not created for death. God had another tree in the garden besides the one that gave knowledge of good and evil. It was a tree that gave eternal life. He knew if we ate from that tree before redemption, we would be eternally separated from God. Death ushered in the possibility of resurrected life, untainted by sin, that was eternal.

Like those who attempt to lessen the evil of sin, only to lessen the meaning of grace, those who lessen the need to mourn inadvertently lessen the joy of resurrection. If we say the law is no big deal, then the gospel is just optional. If we say the law is severe, the gospel rises up to meet it.

To paraphrase G.K. Chesterton, fairy tales don't tell children about dragons, they've known dragons for as long as they've had an imagination. Fairy tales tell children that there is a knight to slay the dragon.[3] It is wise to apply that logic. To deny the existence of the "dragon" in people's life is to deny the knight coming to kill it. There is a difference between living in hope and expectation, and feeling shame that you aren't excited yet. Lament is a spiraling of pain and emotions, a torrent inside our souls. Truth grounds us. Truth centers us. Don't tell me about the resurrection when you deny the pain of death.

The law gives meaning to the gospel. Work gives meaning to rest. Death gives meaning to the resurrection. If we are to extol the glory of the gospel, the glory of rest, or the glory of the resurrection, we must not minimize what it is conquering. We must allow those who mourn to mourn, so that we have a firm grasp of what Jesus conquered. He reaches into the depth of *that kind* of pain to redeem us.

We are told that the reality of the resurrection is where we find our hope. We are told that Jesus has had victory over death. Some say we should celebrate victory, and we will. God is more patient than our peers, as Job also learned.

After my miscarriage, I posted about it online and received condolences. Then there was Libby. She was a friend I met online in a sewing forum. We had known each other online for a few years, and we connected especially because we were both Christians from similar backgrounds.

When Libby, who lived 4 hours away found out about my miscarriage, she packed up her things and she and her husband and 2 kids drove out to our farm which was in full harvest mode with my husband's long hours in the field. Her kids ran off to play with my kids, and her husband rode in the combine with my husband, and we just talked. Then her family took me and my kids out to a restaurant. She and her husband ordered for my kids and attended to all of their needs, cutting food and wiping hands. "I want you to just sit there and eat. Don't do anything," she told me.

I ordered a bacon cheeseburger, and with the first bite, I realized for the first time in 2 days that I had not eaten anything. It felt like every cell in my body suddenly started crying out for food. My grief had been so consuming that I hadn't eaten, and I hadn't even realized it. I needed someone to come to my home, care for my children, and say, "you just sit there and eat. Here is the food." We can't mourn in isolation. It's in isolation when we get stuck. In lament, we need someone to do what needs to be done. No one understands this better than God.

Mourning is individualistic, in that no one can walk through it for you, and it is communal, because we are called to mourn with those who mourn. There is strength in the numbers of mourners. It didn't even have to happen to you, it doesn't even need to be your loss, and yet you are called to mourn with others. When you are feeling the most insane and out of your senses, you need to be surrounded by people who confirm you are not out of your mind. The reality is this is awful. "This is an *enormous* loss. I'm so sorry you're grieving something so precious." They confirm the loss when we are disoriented, and they confirm the value of what was lost, so that our pain is acknowledged.

To go to a funeral for the sake of the grieving, to send condolences, bring a meal, and comfort those who are experiencing loss of any kind is training us to acknowledge to others in our world that we need a Savior. It acknowledges to the world that morals are not enough, good works won't save us. Death will come no matter what. We cannot outmaneuver it.

God deals with us in truth. It is good to acknowledge that which is true. It's good to acknowledge hurt and wrong done. We feel like we're dying from grief, but the breath of God keeps filling our lungs.

Mourning is slow. It's like trying to run in deep water. In a world that offers prepackaged, pre-processed food, ideas, and mottos, mourning is slow. No one can process grief for you, and we cannot delegate it. If you delay mourning, it will come back like a boomerang and insist it not be skipped. Through it all, lament can feel like you're backed into a corner to ask the questions of God we had previously not dared to ask. In mourning, our reservations and pretenses are removed and we expose to God what we really think. We ask from the deepest part of our souls, new places we didn't know had been simmering below the surface for years. We will no longer be satisfied by mottos. We want answers.

I think one of the reasons why we fear lament is that we fear offending God with our questions and our anger. We fear that it will all slip out, and we are trying to keep it together to please him. We want to appear obedient and pious. We want to know the correct answers to life's toughest questions. But when we are in lament, the gloves are off. Who knows what we'll say? What we really think, lies we weren't even conscious of believing, come to the surface as we lack the strength to hold it back anymore. In lament, it all comes to the light.

It's not that all types of mourning are holy. Of course, we can cross lines and say some pretty irreverent things. But mourning doesn't cause the doubt and lies, it brings them to the surface. What we don't realize is that God isn't scared of our questions, and he's already conquered our sin. He's not scared of our anger. He is after our hearts, and in mourning, the full state of all of it is exposed for us to see in his presence. As 1 John 1 talks about walking in the light, this is exactly where God wants us to be. It's not that he wants us to sin. It's that he wants us to be honest. God has no interest in pretend relationships.

As mourning is slow, our patience does not feel sufficient for the cause. God often seems silent. God is not our puppet, and he does not respond with the words we sometimes want to hear. For the older saints who have known mourning multiple times, they have seen the other side. They have seen God's faithfulness from the other side. But for those just starting out, the silence feels like it could go on forever. This is when we learn to wait upon the Lord. This is when we learn to sit in expectation, we learn to hope, and we learn that faith is a certainty of things we do not yet see. We are so horrible at it, but the only reason that it does grow us is that God's patience outlasts ours.

A Picture of Our Father

I have said before and it continues to be true, that my husband has been a huge source of healing in my life. Seeing him be a father to our children is healing for me, as I had a more complicated relationship with my own father. My husband has a broad chest, strong arms, and being a fourth-generation farmer, he has huge working-man hands that can hold a child still without much effort. But his patience seems unending. Occasionally, when the children are little, they will be in such a tantrum that he will hold them, and they will beat against his chest, and scream into his face, and their scrawny little arms and legs flail, because something isn't what it should have been, and something isn't how they want it, and they cannot handle it. He will hold them gently, and often hum or sing into their ear. They will push and fight, and he holds them in a hug as they struggle, waiting for them to be calmed by his strength. It takes a while.

Some children struggle more than others. The father is patient. He's waiting until they relax into his love. We breathe in the breath of God and slowly let it out with a quiver.

God will not punish us for mourning. In fact, he meets us there. He is there holding us while we flail around, knowing we have to get it out, acknowledging that things aren't as they should be. We do not plan to mourn, but God will use it to train us. We cannot and should not avoid mourning, as it will lessen our understanding of what the resurrection means. God sees the bigger picture, as he so graphically tells Job in the end of his book. But God did respond to Job, when the time was right. He didn't give him the answer, but he told Job a lot about himself in the process, which in the end was more valuable.

So many days we want the gospel without the law that showed us our need. We want the resurrection without its preceding death. We want the victory without the battle. We are too afraid to sit in pain. We are afraid it will consume us, so we run and hide from it.

Oftentimes, healing is found in calling something what it is, saying what needs to be said, and seeing what needs to be seen. Our job in Eden was to name things. Sometimes that's all we can do, and it is sacred. Sometimes we need to face our pain in order to see the ridiculousness of it. Sometimes we need to face our pain so that the lies it's been telling us can be called out. Sometimes we need to face our pain just to see that the breath of God still flows in and out of our lungs, and it did not in fact kill us.

We want so badly for "it is finished" to mean "now skip to the end." We have to put together the pieces of how the resurrection changes everything that matters in our lives, and in the process the Holy Spirit will carry a hope for a new day. His mercies are new every morning. He is faithful.

CHAPTER 15

Discipleship

"And Jesus came and said to them, 'All authority in heaven and on earth has been given to me. Go therefore and make disciples of all nations, baptizing them in the name of the Father and of the Son and of the Holy Spirit, teaching them to observe all that I have commanded you. And behold, I am with you always, to the end of the age."

—MATTHEW 28:18–20

WE OFTEN FEAR DISCIPLESHIP. Most of us don't mind the idea of being discipled by someone else. Who wouldn't like a mother figure or father figure to bring our troubles to, and sort out what's going on in our lives and in the world—someone who will always point us back to Christ? But going out and making disciples sounds demanding. It sounds like stretching your comfort zone to the limit. It sounds like a job for people who study apologetics, and have degrees and ordinations and lots and lots of experience. You know, people with the "spiritual gift" of discipleship.

Making disciples doesn't really even make it onto the "list" of those who are exhausted in any sense of the word. It's something that those in the church often delegate to the professionals.

I have often equated discipleship with the apologetic debates that happen at universities—an argument. I have to defend my faith. It feels like it would be a battle. God has certainly called individuals for such events, but that's not what I would consider discipleship.

Discipleship first and foremost begins within relationships. You're calling someone to be with you, in your life, or you're going to be with someone else in their life. You share your life with them, because you want them to see how God has changed your life.

Discipleship is often seen as benefiting those who are being discipled, but I have found discipleship relationships to be mutually beneficial. I have always felt like I receive more than I give. There is something about sharing what God has done for me again and again, in various contexts that has rooted my own faith in remembrance of the works of God. It's a privilege to witness someone's face change—witness their whole lives change because of something you said about God. The joy is indescribable.

I don't want to say something like "there is no excuse for not discipling," applying pressure, ultimatums, or guilt for hesitating to disciple another. But I do want to express that in calling you to make disciples, God is not wishing to harm you. His call to discipleship is good. It will surprise you in rewarding ways that you will only realize as you walk through it. As you share with someone else God's faithfulness in your own life, you'll be comforted by the memory.

That's right. He has been faithful.

When you are asked a question that you actually know the answer to, you'll realize how far God has brought you. When you speak over someone in pain with words that you didn't know you had, and see how the life in front of you is changed, you'll be shocked that the Holy

Spirit would put those words in your mouth, and it will bring you to your knees in worship.

I can't tell you what God will do, or how he will do it. But I know that the call to discipleship is a gift we don't deserve. Discipling others, the relationships formed, the front row seat to God at work in another person's life, has been one of the greatest treasures and encouragements that God has given me.

What to Teach, How to Teach

Knowing what to teach them, and how to answer questions is often a big stress point. I take a very classical approach. The classical approach is called the "Trivium" and was used from ancient times to describe how the human brain learns. Like the Trinity, it has three parts, and in fact, the early church often explained the Trinity to philosophers by using the Trivium as an example. Without reading too much into it, I'm putting the person in the Trinity who they said was connected to that stage of learning, for the value of a mnemonic device.

Stage 1: Grammar (Father)

In this stage of learning, people learn what is. It is the stage of facts, memorization, reading direct source texts, (reading the Bible, rather than books about the Bible), storytelling, and passing down memories or experiences. This is the stage where biblical literacy is developed, when people learn Bible stories, and they start committing some of the stories or verses to memory. The focus of this stage isn't to explain what everything means, but to expose them to what is. What is truth? This is the story of God. This is what God actually said. He is who he is.

Stage 2: Logic (Son)

This is a big connecting phase. We learn how the pieces of information fit together. What is their relationship? Was there a cause and effect? What was the circumstance? What was the context? How does it compare to other parts of the Bible? How does it relate to other parts of the Bible? Where is Christ in this story? What happened before this? What happened after this? What was going on at the same time? How does this apply to me? Is this information reliable? Is this law, or is this gospel? While people can learn facts in isolation, classical teachers agree that people cannot go through the logic phase in isolation. It requires another person to work through these facts. It requires a community to some degree. This stage is largely done in conversation.

Step 3: Rhetoric (Holy Spirit)

This is the stage where we speak or express what we know to be true. The ones who were discipled learn to go and make disciples. This is the stage of missionaries, pastors, artists, musicians, poets, writers, and mothers explaining as carefully as they can what they know to be true. Keeping in mind how people hear things and expressing it with a desire to speak the truth as clearly as possible, this stage is an expression of what we know that can be so powerful that it changes the world. This is when we learn what it is to love our neighbor.

For instance, say you wanted to teach someone the book of Luke. Step one would be to read the actual text with them and tell them the story. Perhaps together you pick verses or whole chapters to memorize together. Next, you compare this text to other texts. Compare this account to other accounts. Compare it to the Old Testament.

Learn how to distinguish passages talking about law and passages talking about gospel.

Finally, when the spark of connection hits this person, they will be compelled to express it. Perhaps they want to tell others how the book of Luke changed their lives. Perhaps they want to say how they saw things they've never seen before. Perhaps they will write a song about it, write a Bible study, draw a painting, tell the story to their child, or express their knowledge that is too good to keep to themselves.

Too often, we are trying to manufacture excitement for evangelism and discipleship outside of this model. We rely on formulas, filling out cards, and bringing them step by step through a series of doors and verses. "You don't have to know anything, just follow these instructions and say these words" like some multilevel marketing company's plan for success. Making disciples involves exposing them to the truth, having a conversation about it as they process, being a safe place for them to wrestle and say stupid things, and bearing witness to the awakening that the Holy Spirit gives, as they are baptized into the truth. They cannot unsee what they have seen.

And this process never stops. We never grow out of our need to be discipled. There are always parts of the Bible we haven't studied, parts we don't yet understand, or ideas of God we are still trying to wrap our heads around. We go back to stage one whenever we are exposed to new information, whenever we read and study a new book of the Bible, or we hear a verse in a new way. We are exposed to what is truth, we process and test that truth, and then that truth plays out in our lives in a way that edifies and builds up those around us.

In this process, wrestling with the truth and the privilege of expressing that truth is our only participation. Stories are given to you. Conversation is given to you. Understanding is given to you. That is the process of being a disciple.

Not in a Place to Disciple

In my situation, sometimes the only people I'm discipling are the little people in my home. I teach them the stories. I stay up late and have the conversations. It wasn't until I felt the pull to disciple others that I started to really question God's sanity or try to explain to him that I wasn't in a good place right now.

As I thought about making disciples outside those God put under my care in the home, I didn't want my kids to ever feel like their needs or questions were impeding ministry; I wanted them to know their souls had value as well, and they were absolutely part of my vocation. I probably went too far in the other direction, as pendulums swing, and pretty soon, as my children grew older, they started to think I existed to serve them and only them. Getting involved in ministry and discipleship was something other families did. My job was to keep them as comfortable as possible, they thought.

It was then that I started praying for God to bring our family to some kind of informal ministry within our church. I started praying that God would lead me to people to disciple. He led me to some Christians in need of hearing the gospel afresh, and some non-Christians, who had serious questions about what the gospel actually was.

My biggest issue was time. I had none. I was already overloaded. I prayed about that too. I wasn't sure what to drop. It was quickly shown to me that I had between 7–8:30 am available every other week. So, I started inviting people God laid on my heart out to coffee. Then I spent a lot of time listening. Like the passage in Titus 2, I wanted to be an older woman who was trustworthy. It would take time for them to see I wouldn't gossip about them, and time for them to gauge whether or not I had discernment.

Right around the six-month mark in each of these relationships, things started to tumble out. Each one of the women I met with had a firm grammar foundation of knowing the Bible, but they didn't have a lot of experience with having someone to ask the hard questions. I often said, "that's an excellent and valid question. Even I don't know the answer but let me look into it." Or "I have thought the same thing too. I think I know who we can ask about this."

I wanted them to know it's okay to not always know. There is no shame in that. Sometimes we must be content to wonder.

My goal in these meetings wasn't to train these women to live better, more moral lives, or to teach them to homeschool like I homeschooled, or tell them they had to stay at home like I stayed at home. My goal was for them to know God and be a witness to God working in their lives.

Still another time, there was a single woman who dropped into my life. For much of her childhood, God had been used against her, and she desired to know God, but she had a lot of trust issues. She had almost no grammar knowledge of the stories of God, or the actual word of God. In this case, I had to recognize that she didn't even have information to connect together. We needed to go back to the basics and learn the stories. We talked a lot about the law and gospel, which touched her the most because even grace had been turned into a law in her childhood home.

A lot of reading. A lot of discussion. A lot of patience. A lot of follow up. She became my friend. When she was over at our house, my kids would be better behaved at supper, and I would wonder, "why did I think this would be hard?" She would consciously spend time with each of my kids by reading them a story, or she would talk to me about my day. She witnessed me disciplining, witnessed my husband and I work through an argument, witnessed my children meltdown.

"I really liked how you handled that," she would tell me afterwards. I always felt exhausted after any of those things happened, but for a non-Christian to see me do it and say "So, tell me why you did it this way. Where did you learn that?" It built me up, but also opened a door for yet another conversation.

There are times when you encounter someone angry. The pain that Satan has inflicted on many in the name of God runs deep. I don't try to change hearts. Trying to manipulate the heart is a fool's errand, and constantly frustrating. I can only speak the truth in love. Subtract the love, and it ceases to be the whole truth. Subtract the truth, and I'm just giving people good feelings or "vibes."

But at its core, discipleship is giving bread to people who are starving. With patience and prayer, it is one of my most favorite things to do. It shows me on a consistent basis that God is at work in others. I witness hearts change that I didn't think could change. Discipleship builds my faith in ways that nothing else does.

Start with Prayer

I don't want to go where God has not sent me. I don't want to say what God has not called me to say. I don't want to overreach and think that I have the capacity, with my intellect, my persuasion, and my gifting to change the world. I've been down that road, and it damaged me severely.

I don't want any of that anymore. Therefore, any move to discipleship has to begin with prayer. "God, show me. Make it as clear as can be for someone as dense as I am what you want me to do, and what you want me to say. I want the Holy Spirit directing every move." When I pray this, things happen, and I don't get puffed with pride, I get filled with wonder at what I got to see God do. When I understand my limitations, it makes every encounter a miracle that he did in spite of my limitations.

So much damage has been done over the course of church history when Christians have forced discipleship, demanding that we force others to believe *now* and shoving the Bible down their throats.

Discipleship can become a misuse of power. It's when we say, "God told us to do this, and we will get it done one way or the other." We are patient because we know that only the Holy Spirit has the power to change hearts, and faith comes through hearing the word. We just have to share his word, without manipulation, without rushing, but with love and patience. Because we know the Holy Spirit will draw them to Christ, or he will not, in his time. God has restricted our knowledge of a lot of his timing, and perhaps this is why. We don't need to know, because if we did, we would use it to manipulate hearts, and changing hearts has always been his job.

But over the years, we see it happen, again, and again. When we see the understanding wash over their face, when we see the wonder of God's love grip their hearts, and we get to be there to see it— nothing else helps you understand the faithfulness of God like seeing a changed heart.

This does not mean that you are guaranteed to see someone come to faith for the first time. But when you are discipling others, even those who are already in the faith, by discipling them in his word, you can witness them growing in their understanding in faith.

Every one of the spiritual disciplines in this book play into this. You cannot disciple without prayer. You cannot teach if you don't know Scriptures. Understanding your lack will help you see his strength. The repetition of confessing will remind you of his grace that does not run dry. Through learning to lament, you will disciple with compassion instead of arrogance. All of these things are the Holy Spirit shaping you and forming you for his kingdom's purposes— to pour the truth and substance of his love on others. But when it comes down to it, you realize that, as he teaches you to love him and love others, you're brought to your knees in worship, at the greatness of his love.

Notes

Chapter 1

1. Rachel Joy Welcher, "Storm Garden," in *Two Funerals, Then Easter* (Glenwood, IA: Dustlings Press, 2018), 37.

2. Robert E. Webber, *Worship Old and New* (Grand Rapids, MI: Zondervan, 1994), 14. *Worship Old and New* by Copyright © 1994 by Robert E. Webber. Used by permission of Zondervan. www.zondervan.com.

Chapter 2

1. Jared Wilson, *The Imperfect Disciple* (Grand Rapids, MI: Baker Books, 2017), 25.

Chapter 3

1. JD Greear, *Jesus, Continued* (Grand Rapids, MI: Zondervan, 2014), 78.

2. Warren Olsen and David Rinden, eds., *An Explanation of Luther's Small Catechism*, 2nd ed. (Fergus Falls, MN: Faith and Fellowship Press, 1988), 84.

3. Martin Luther, *The Freedom of the Christian*, trans. Mark Tranvik (Minneapolis, MN: Fortress Press, 2008), 71–72.

4. Luther, *Freedom of the Christian*, 74.

5. Bryan Chapell, *Holiness by Grace: Delighting in the Joy That is Our Strength* (Wheaton, IL: Crossway, 2011), 20.

Chapter 4

1. Douglas McKelvey, *Every Moment Holy* (Nashville, TN: Rabbit Room Press, 2017), 159.

2. Kevin S. Krahenbuhl, "Science on Learning: The Limits of Memory," *CiRCE Institute*, September 14, 2018, https://www.circeinstitute.org/blog/science-learning-limits-memory.

3. Stratford Caldecott, *Beauty in the Word: Rethinking the Foundations of Education* (Tacoma, WA: Angelico Press, 2012), 44.

4. Caldecott, *Beauty in the Word*, 44.

5. Leland Ryken, James C. Wilhoit, and Tremper Longman III, eds., *Dictionary of Biblical Imagery* (Downers Grove, IL: InterVarsity Press, 1998), s.v. "remembrance."

6. Luther, *Freedom of the Christian*, 71.

7. Warren Olsen and David Rinden, eds., *An Explanation of Luther's Small Catechism*, 2nd ed. (Fergus Falls, MN: Faith and Fellowship Press, 1988), 75.

8. *An Explanation of Luther's Small Catechism*, 76.

9. *An Explanation of Luther's Small Catechism*, 84.

Chapter 5

1. Luther, *Freedom of the Christian*, vii.

2. Luther, *Freedom of the Christian*, vii.

3. Sarah Bessey, "The (Successful) Pursuit of God: Family, Work, Ministry, and the Ghost of A.W. Tozer," *Fathom Magazine*, October 23, 2019, https://www.fathommag.com/stories/the-successful-pursuit-of-god.

Chapter 6

1. Martin Luther, *Luther's Works: Career of the Reformer III*, Volume 33, ed. Philip S. Watson (Minneapolis, MN: Fortress Press, 1957), 24.

Chapter 7

1. Wendell Berry, "1979, X: Whatever is foreseen in joy," in *This Day: Collected and New Sabbath Poems* (Berkley, CA: Counterpoint Press, 2014), 20, st. 2. Copyright © 2013 by Wendell Berry, from *This Day: Collected and New Sabbath Poems*. Reprinted by permission of Counterpoint Press.

2. Emily P. Freeman, "Keep Your Rest," June 5, 2018, in *The Next Right Thing*, podcast, MP3 audio, 14:13, https://emilypfreeman.com/podcast/the-next-right-thing/40/.

3. Justin Martyr, "The First Apology of Justin," in *The Ante-Nicene Fathers: The Apostolic Fathers, Justin Martyr, Iranaeus*, Volume 1, eds. Alexander Roberts and James Donaldson, 1885, republished in *Christian Classics Ethereal Library*, Chapter LXVII.

4. Justin Martyr, "Dialogue with Trypho," in *The Ante-Nicene Fathers*, Chapter XXI.

5. Justin Martyr, "Dialogue with Trypho," in *The Ante-Nicene Fathers*, Chapter XXIII.

6. John Koessler, *The Radical Pursuit of Rest* (Downers Grove, IL: InterVarsity Press, 2016), 16.

Chapter 8

1. Martin Luther, *Martin Luther's Basic Theological Writings*, 3rd ed., W.R. Russell and T.F. Lull, eds. (Minneapolis, MN: Fortress Press, 2012), 292–294.

2. Dietrich Bonhoeffer, *Life Together* (New York, NY: HarperCollins, 1954), 74.

Chapter 9

1. Flannery O'Conner, *A Prayer Journal*, ed. Mary Flannery O'Conner (New York, NY: Farrar, Strause and Giroux, 2013), 7.

2. Martin Luther, *A Simple Way to Pray: For Peter, the Master Barber*, trans. Matthew C. Harrison (St. Louis, MO: Concordia Publishing House, 2012), 6.

3. Caldecott, *Beauty in the Word*, 44.

Chapter 10

1. J.I. Packer, *Knowing God* (Downers Grove, IL: InterVarsity Press, 1973), 23.

2. John W. Kleinig, *Grace Upon Grace: Spirituality for Today* (St. Louis, MO: Concordia Publishing House, 2008), 21.

3. Kleinig, *Grace Upon Grace*, 21.

4. Kleinig, *Grace Upon Grace*, 22.

5. Kleinig, *Grace Upon Grace*, 21.

6. Kleinig, *Grace Upon Grace*, 20.

7. C.S. Lewis, *Surprised by Joy* (San Francisco, CA: Harper One, 2017), 172.

8. Sarah Clarkson, *Caught Up in a Story* (Monument, CO: Storyformed Books, 2013), 21.

Chapter 11

1. David Mathis, *Habits of Grace: Enjoying Jesus through the Spiritual Disciplines* (Wheaton, IL: Crossway, 2016), 121–122.

2. 2 Sam. 12:16, 1 Kgs. 21:9, 1 Kgs. 21:12, 2 Chr. 20:3, Ezra 8:21, Neh. 9:1, Esth. 4:3, Ps. 35:13, 69:10, 109:24, Isa. 58:5–6, Jer. 36:6, 9, Dan. 9:3, Joel 1:14, 2:12, 15, Jonah 3:5, Zec. 8:19.

3. *Dictionary of Biblical Imagery*, s.v. "fasting."

Chapter 12

1. Bonhoeffer, *Life Together*, 118.

2. Bonhoeffer, *Life Together*, 112.

Chapter 14

1. C.S. Lewis, *A Grief Observed* (San Francisco, CA: HarperCollins, 1996), 3.

2. Welcher, "First Three Months," in *Two Funerals, Then Easter*, 110.

3. G.K. Chesterton, *Tremendous Trifles* (Urbana, IL: Project Gutenburg, 2009), Chapter XVIII: The Tower. https://www.gutenberg.org/files/8092/8092-h/8092-h.htm.

Made in the USA
Monee, IL
08 November 2023